SEX, DEATH, & THE ANGRY YOUNG MAN

Conversations with Riane Eisler & David Loye

by Mathew Callahan

Some of this material originally appeared in *Komotion International Live & Kicking*, San Francisco, numbers 3 and 4.

Selected excerpts of text from *The Chalice and the Blade* by Riane Eisler. Copyright © 1987 by Riane Eisler. Reprinted by permission of HarperCollins Publishers Inc.

Typesetting, collages, and design were graciously donated by Freddie Baer, who shepherded the presentation from the initial articles to book form.

First printing

Times Change Press: P.O. Box 1380, Ojai CA 93024
Sales office: c/o Publishers Services, Box 2510, Novato CA 94948

Printed by workers under union contract.

Library of Congress Cataloging-in-Publication Data

Callahan, Mathew, 1951-
    Sex, death, and the angry young man : conversations with Riane Eisler and David Loye / by Mathew Callahan.
        p.   cm.
    Includes bibliographical references.
    ISBN 0-87810-040-7 (paper) : $8.50
    1. Eisler, Riane Tennenhaus. Chalice and the blade. 2. Sex role--History. 3. Social evolution--History. 4. Patriarchy--History. 5. Social history.   I. Eisler, Riane Tennenhaus. II. Loye, David. III. Title.
HQ1075.C35   1993
305.3'09--dc20   93-21468
                                                      CIP

This book, including the cover, is printed on recycled paper.

Table of Contents

Introduction _____ 7

Sex, Death, and the Angry Young Man

Violence and Conflict _____ 13
Art: Deconstruction and Reconstruction _____ 25
Constructive Anger _____ 37
Ethnicity and Moral Sensitivity _____ 40
The Shift from Partnership to Domination _____ 43
Paradigm Shifts and Their Texts _____ 50
Anarchism and Partnership _____ 55
Sex, Connectedness, and Nurturance _____ 63
Getting from Here to Partnership _____ 70

Biographical Conversations

Riane Eisler _____ 87
David Loye _____ 100

Resources

Glossary _____ 113
Suggested Readings _____ 116
Connections _____ 118

This gylanic world . . . will be a world where limitations and fear will no longer be systematically taught us through myths about how inevitably evil and perverse we humans are. In this world, children will not be taught epics about men who are honored for being violent or fairy tales about children who are lost in frightful woods where women are malevolent witches. They will be taught new myths, epics, and stories in which human beings are good; men are peaceful; and the power of creativity and love — symbolized by the sacred Chalice, the holy vessel of life — is the governing principle. For in this gylanic world, our drive for justice, equality, and freedom, our thirst for knowledge and spiritual illumination, and our yearning for love and beauty will be at last be freed. And after the bloody detour of andocratic history, both women and men will at last find out what being human can mean.

Introduction

It's New Year's Day 1991. As dusk gathers I turn the final page of *The Chalice and the Blade*. A light snow is falling over the south rim of the Grand Canyon, a suitably portentous setting for the contemplation of the fate of humanity and the planet we inhabit. Writing this now, I almost expect the background music to swell, the clouds to part, and an angel to descend from the heavens, beckoning me to heed the call of a higher authority! But, in fact, I was welcoming the first year of the last decade of the millennium looking out upon contradictions: incredible vistas polluted by smog from neighboring power plants, winter winds carrying birds whose calls were drowned out by the sounds of automobiles and tour buses — a few stolen moments away from the hard asphalt and dark nights that envelop me and the taxi I drive for a living.

No, the revelation was not in the Word. It was in the experience. It was and it is. It is not given. It is fought for and grappled with, shaped and twisted out of the solid rock of real life. Then, just when you think you've got it down, the great roulette wheel of chance calls your number and the music they're playing is in 7/8 and the dance you've spent your whole life learning, for this very moment, is in 4/4! But dance you must. Not the one you intended, not the one you planned for. But a living, breathing dance nonetheless.

This has been my experience. This is how I got to that place at that time.

I am a musician. My grandmother was a dancer of the Isadora Duncan generation and tradition. My mother followed in her footsteps (no pun intended). Both were involved in the social movements of their times. Reds. I was raised in the dancing school my grandmother and her elder sister founded in San Francisco in 1912, Peters-Wright Creative Dance. It continues today under my mother's direction.

I rebelled against everything. I left home the day after I got out of high school and ever since have been surviving alternately as a musician, stevedore, factory worker, and, now, cab driver. I can't remember when I didn't consider myself a revolutionary. I'm in a band called the Looters and I am a founding member of an artists' collective called Komotion International. The Looters were born in a basement on Rose Street in San Francisco's Fillmore District. We combine the do-it-yourself spirit of punk with the cultural diversity of the city we grew up in to make rhythms for dancing across a minefield. Komotion is the effort of many artists of different disciplines, and provides a place to work and perform outside the polluted waters of the mainstream.

I love my mother and I love my life, so what do I have to complain about when so many people are so miserable? Because I know that anything good that has happened in or around me has been in spite of the Death Culture. I refuse to allow the purveyors of hypocrisy and enslavement to take credit for that which the people have wrenched from their bloody grip. Any little happiness, any little joy, is our creation, not some privileged potentate's! When I perform a song and people are inspired to face another day it's not because the government allowed me to do it. It's not because I have the right. It's because I see and I do and there are others with whom I share that, and we come together to form a community not defined by those we hate but by those we love. We don't need to create an identity by branding some social group that looks different "The Other." We base our life and work on building the kinds of social relations that embody our ideals. No one's going to sell me that that's the American Way. Having worked with people from literally all over the world, I know that that's the human way, or it's no way at all.

I read *The Chalice and the Blade* critically. In fact, I attacked and dissected it from every angle I could think of. I had to conclude that it is quite possibly, as Ashley Montagu said, "the most important book since Darwin's *Origin of Species*." But I also knew that the true test of its significance was its ability to inspire debate amongst those actively trying to transform society. That means challenging people to take up every social question as their own responsibility and not to rely on experts or intellectuals to do their thinking for them. It means situating this in a historical context: understanding where these ideas come from and how much all of us are indebted to the struggles of our predecessors throughout the world. It is important to reject prevailing categorizations such as "Western thought," because the battlefront has been global for at least several centuries and has included slaves resisting masters regardless of ancestry or geography. It is vital that people not territorialize and commodify experience or thinking. This is how we lose our lives.

What needs to be illuminated are the myriad ways in which our experience and aspirations are bound together. How our common interests are marginalized and buried beneath a mountain of rotting garbage. How quickly gigantic changes can happen in an unstable system. What place reason has in the life of the people and how we are discouraged from using it. Who "we" are after ten thousand years of domination.

It is in this spirit that these conversations took place and are to be shared. If they raise more questions, good. If they help to inform action, better. But beyond dogma and orthodoxy lie experiment and understanding. And, if we do well, then beyond the time of the dominator may lie the time of transformation for our species.

***

The Chalice and the Blade is a challenge. Published by HarperSanFrancisco in 1987, it has received a worldwide readership, including translation into nine languages, and continues to spark discussion and debate. In the second issue of *Komotion International Live & Kicking* I wrote an article, "Illusions of Strength in the Time of the Dominator," which took up some of the ideas in that book in an attempt to shed some light on the profound problems I encountered in the struggle against the Gulf War. In a fortuitous meeting, I gave Riane Eisler, the book's author, and her life partner, David Loye — co-author with her of *The Partnership Way* — a copy of the magazine and requested an interview. What follows is based on two lengthy, wide-ranging dialogues that took place in July 1991 and August 1992.

— MATHEW CALLAHAN

A NOTE

In these conversations, there is frequent reference to three terms — *gylany* and the *dominator* and *partnership* models — introduced by Riane Eisler in *The Chalice and the Blade*. While the definitions of other unusual terms will be found in this book's glossary, I thought it would be helpful to quote introductory statements relating to these three before the conversations actually begin:

"To describe the real alternative to a system based on the ranking of half of humanity over the other, I propose the new term *gylany* [pronounced GUY-la-nee]. *Gy* derives from the Greek root word *gyne* or "woman." *An* derives from *andros* or "man." The letter *l* between the two has a double meaning. In English, it stands for the *linking* of both halves of humanity, rather than, as in androcracy, their ranking. In Greek, it derives from the verb *lyein* or *lyo*, which in turn has a double meaning: to solve or resolve (as in ana*ly*sis) and to dissolve or set free (as in cata*ly*sis). In this sense, the letter *l* stands for the resolution of our problems through the freeing of both halves of humanity from the stultifying and distorting rigidity of roles imposed by the domination hierarchies inherent in androcratic systems." (*The Chalice and the Blade*, p. 105.)

". . . [U]nderlying the great surface diversity of human culture are two basic models of society.

"The first, which I call the *dominator* model, is what is popularly termed either patriarchy or matriarchy — the *ranking* of one half of humanity over the other. The second, in which social relations are primarily based on the principle of *linking* rather than ranking, may best be described as the *partnership* model. In this model — beginning with the most fundamental difference in our species, between male and female — diversity is not equated with either inferiority or superiority." (*The Chalice and the Blade*, p. xvii.)

M.C.

A note on the format:
Mathew Callahan's questions and comments are set in **bold**.

To describe the real alternative to a system based on the ranking of half of humanity over the other, I propose the new term *gylany*. *Gy* derives from the Greek root word *gyne*, or "woman." *An* derives from *andros*, or "man." The letter *l* between the two has a double meaning. In English, it stands for the *linking* of both halves of humanity, rather than, as in androcracy, their ranking. In Greek it derives from the verb *lyein* or *lyo*, which in turn has a double meaning: to solve or resolve (as in analysis) and to dissolve or set free (as in catalysis). In this sense, the letter *l* stands for the resolution of our problems through the freeing of both halves of humanity from the stultifying and distorting rigidity of roles imposed by the domination hierarchies inherent in androcratic systems.

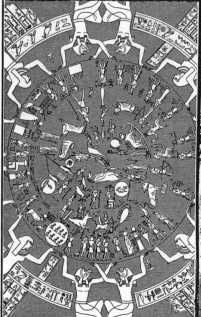

Sex, Death,
and the Angry Young Man

Violence and Conflict

We were talking about my article in issue two of *Komotion International Live & Kicking*, which dealt with opposing the Gulf War and with the need for rebellion that must include the reclaiming of joy and the celebration of life. . . .

Riane Eisler: I was very interested in your discussion of the rebellion of the sons against the fathers, of the young men against the old men. How on the surface it looks like it's going to change something, but in the end it reinvigorates what I've called a dominator model of society, where basically it's those who are the angrier, those who have the most vigor, who set the agenda. I loved what you said, that of course they have the power for lifegiving and for feeling and for sensation, but, and this is most important, the way that it's channeled through male socialization is not into that at all. It's into rebellion and through rebellion into taking control and dominating. So you get the second generation of dominators, and it's an illusion that something has basically changed. I think that point is very well taken because the whole male socialization is to see anger as almost a rite of initiation into manhood, when you are permitted to act out your anger (which children and women are not permitted to express). That is the moment when, in a dominator society, you're initiated into the male fraternity of dominators of various ranks. The degree and the circumstances under which you are socially permitted to express and act out that anger will vary according to where you sit in that hierarchy and that particular period in time, but anger is a crucial element of a system that is really ultimately held together by force or the threat of force.

You might say that this is a modern conceit because the French Revolution — the legacy of that period of upheaval — is what brought forth the angry young man of our times, from Arthur Rimbaud to Henry Miller, to Elvis Presley, for that matter. In earlier times you certainly had the dominator model, particularly in Europe with the Catholic Church and the whole hierarchy, and even with the Reformation there were the Calvinists and all of that repressive ideological baggage. How do you think that anger was channeled then?

Riane Eisler: First of all you had war, and male anger was channeled through the male as warrior, the young male as warrior. Then you had an endless series of scapegoatings, like the witch-hunts and the Crusades. And we still have that scapegoating, whether it is antisemitism or racial or ethnic persecutions. Then there was, as there still is, male anger in the home. Brutality and violence in the family were very widespread — and still are. You have legacies of that in phrases like "spare the rod and spoil the child." The physical chastisement of children was considered to be proper, not only by men but also by women, who served, and still serve, as agents for dominator socialization. But physical chastisement in the home, as in the larger society, was primarily a male prerogative.

So there were always a lot of institutionally sanctioned outlets for male anger. And a lot of excuses like, "He's drunk, that's why he beat her." But actually oppression was socially sanctioned, as Shakespeare's *The Taming of the Shrew* makes clear.

The famous "rule of thumb" comes from a legal reform that the stick with which a man could beat his wife could be no thicker than his thumb.

Such laws governed the relations of men and women in the family — just like the relations between master and slave. In fact, when the American South became a slaveholding society, the slave laws were modeled on the laws governing the status of women.

The French Revolution, the American Revolution, the Age of Enlightenment. . . . Is it really just a continuing saga?

Riane Eisler: Yes and no. First of all I want to say that certainly there were some gains out of the so-called "rights of man" movement (and it was specifically the rights of men; it really did not deal with women or children), even though the American Revolution was a revolution of propertied males, and to a very large extent came about because of economic factors. Still, the revolutionary ideology, while limited to one-half of the population — and even a very small percentage of that half, said that men have certain unalienable rights. That was very definitely a challenge to the dominator premises, where the great virtues were fealty, obedience, and knowing your place in rigid social hierarchies.

The use of violence in order to achieve those rights in a sense democratized the expression of anger on a mass scale. Similarly, we hear a lot about consumerism today, but consumerism in many ways is a democratization of excessive and pointless consumption, which has characterized dominator elites since remote antiquity.

Yes, there were some positive changes and there was some democratization. But it was a very peculiar democratization; it never really dealt with the foundations of a basically undemocratic system based on domination and held together by institutionalized violence.

What I'm saying is that if you're talking about a dominator system, which is what my work deals with, you're talking about a certain configuration. What happens in the family, what happens in the workplace (there was a lot of brutality in the workplace in earlier times, and there still is in many parts of the world), what happens in the state, and what happens intertribally or internationally are of one cloth. This whole issue of male socialization to equate masculine identity with domination, with conquest and the cultivation of male anger (and the suppression of anger in women and in children, and in "inferior races" — the "happy nigger" mythology, they're not supposed to be angry but be contented), is very much part of the dominator ethos.

People often say men don't have emotions, right? Wrong! In dominator socialization men are very carefully allotted certain emotions: anger, contempt. Those are emotions that are appropriate if you're going to dominate. Women feel sorrow; men are not supposed to cry and are taught not to feel pain. It is nonsense, but it's operant. Jumping to today, that's why so many people are questioning what it means to be a woman, what it means to be a man.

There are two halves of humanity called women and men. And if you start questioning those fundamental roles, then you're getting somewhere because you're really questioning what it means to be human in a fundamental sense. You are questioning, as you did in your article on the Gulf War, some of the basic foundation stones that have so skillfully been kept invisible.

When you speak of the foundations of society you have to talk about class. People talked about a class society even before Marx, but certainly the concept was central to his

work. The *Communist Manifesto* is recommended in your *Partnership Way* among the suggested readings. Still, your vision is actually a critique of the various social revolutionary theories that have come along prior to it, including communism.

Riane Eisler: Including capitalism. If you look at society from the perspective that I'm proposing, using these two configurations or models of what I call the dominator or androcratic and the partnership or gylanic, you see that in many ways both capitalism and socialism challenged some of the dominator premises and institutions. The problem is that they also contained, not only in their implementation but even in their ideology, very, very strong dominator elements. So, let's look at what happened.

The bourgeois revolutions are what brought us republicanism. The American Revolution was a bourgeois revolution; it brought gains. And yes, the communist revolutions brought some gains. I went to the Soviet Union. If you consider that the Russian Empire was a feudal society when the Bolsheviks took over, you cannot negate the fact that there was some progress, even though if you talk to formerly Soviet people today, they may tell you that it was all a total loss as far as they're concerned, which is really an amazing statement.

In each revolution some of the dominator premises and institutions were challenged. For example, in the old feudal dominator system it was not considered honorable to buy real estate. What was considered honorable was that you went next door and you killed your neighbor and took his property!

In that sense, capitalism was a move toward a partnership rather than a dominator model. But then in its tremendous emphasis on male aggression, in its reliance on a dominator family structure, and in its basic hierarchy (there has to be inequality, there has to be inequity), capitalism was not exactly a partnership or gylanic model.

And look at what happened with socialism. The dictatorship of the proletariat says it all, doesn't it? The means were violent to get there and the means continued to be violent, despite some of the add-ons toward the end of Marx's life. He and Engels discovered some of the evidence of these earlier societies I write about in *The Chalice and the Blade*. Engels made the famous statement that the first class oppression is the oppression by men of women. Marx and Engels had such insights, but the matter of male-female relations was totally an add-on, not really integrated into what later happened. But such insights did lead, at least in the Soviet Union, to some attention to the status of women. With Stalin there was a major regression, so nothing changed basically. There was, and to a large extent still is, no foundation for anything except another dominator model. And if you look at all the colonial revolutions — Marxist, non-Marxist, whatever they were—what have you got for the most part? You have the same thing that you did before the colonizers came. For the most part you have strongman rule by an indigenous strongman.

But do you think that such rule is intrinsic to the legacy of Marxism or Leninism?

Riane Eisler: No. No. No.

What Marx and Engels are describing in the *Communist Manifesto* is a classless society in which people live as the true family of man. Of course they used that terminology because that was the legacy of their time, but in modern times I'm sure they would have called it the human family.

Riane Eisler: Yes, I think they would have.

Then in that sense the goal that was being described is not so unlike your own. You could argue about it because people have learned a lot more since then, but the question is, do you think there was something wrong in the way it was gone about, in terms of the actual revolutions, the nature of the struggles? Do you know what I'm saying?

Riane Eisler: Yes. I think both ideology and the means of struggle were at fault. First of all, I think the ideology was still very much a rights-of-man ideology. You have something that is so totally imbalanced that it ignores no less than one-half of the population and doesn't even go into gender issues at all. What we're beginning to understand now is that the phrase "gender issues" really talks about some very fundamental things. It isn't a "woman's issue." We're talking about humans and how humans fundamentally relate. That's item number one about that ideology. Now it depends on what period of Marx you read, but a lot of it is steeped in an ideology that the end does justify the means, violence. And what history shows is that if you use violence, you again institutionalize violence.

How do you define violence then? For instance, nature is clearly violent.

Riane Eisler: Yes, nature is tremendously violent, but it is not necessarily a violence that is institutionalized to maintain a certain social structure—among some animals, yes, and among others, no. I'm very suspicious of any monolithic approach to nature. Nature has a lot of cooperative behavior, symbiotic behavior, synergistic behavior, and also competitive, dominator behavior. Nature has everything in it, and social Darwinism's emphasis on only one aspect of what nature does again reinforces dominator ideology.

The only people who have that ethos of nonviolence—and it's thrust upon them—are women, aren't they? I mean, they're the ones who are supposed to be nonviolent. That's why a movie like *Thelma and Louise* is so strong. As you watched the faces of men going out of the theater, you could see that they were acutely uncomfortable for the most part, though they perhaps could not articulate it. A basic taboo had been shattered. I'm not saying that the answer is for women to start shooting men, or that liberation is the permission that you give yourself to drive off a cliff.

But when she shoots the man who is raping her friend, isn't that justified?

Riane Eisler: What is justified? Sociologically, in terms of the circumstances, the man obviously was a brutal man. But is the solution to his brutality an act of brutality? I would argue no, because I don't think that gets us very far. On a symbolic level, I think it was a very important statement: Hey, women won't take it anymore. And this is a very cruel society to women where they have only one option, which is to drive off a cliff once they basically free themselves from some of their dominations.

But that is not to say that to have women start killing men is the solution to the problem, any more than the solution to their problems has been for the proletariat to rise up violently, or for the bourgeoisie to rise up violently. What I'm really talking about is a culture in which nonviolent conflict resolution is relegated to the most powerless group: women. And I'm saying that if we are really to have a sustainable future—not even a better future, just a sustainable future — given our level of technological development, clearly it's important that nonviolent conflict resolution be something that's part of the socialization of both halves of humanity. I don't have a crystal ball, I don't know how it plays itself out, but I know we have to start with fundamentals.

What I'm asking for is a more useful definition than just the buzzwords *violence* or *nonviolence*.

Riane Eisler: Let's be very specific. While *revolutionary* violence has achieved some limited change, it unfortunately carries within itself the seeds of a system based on violence. That has been one of the great lessons of the twentieth century. It is a tough one for me because I didn't come to this without a long journey, but if I look at revolutionary violence now in terms of systems dynamics, gender issues, the family, and the values that animate and maintain a dominator system, it's just a changing of the guard.

The reason this is such a big issue is because it ties into another area, which is actually cultural. But we don't have to stay on any subject . . .

Riane Eisler: But I'd like to stay on it because, you see, the cultural obsession of the artist, especially the male artist, with violence — the linking of violence and sexuality — actually maintains the system. It looks like a tremendous rebellion. (It's like a little kid saying "fuck." Now I ask you, why should that be a swear word? I mean, we are describing an act of giving and taking pleasure; we are describing an act that in certain circumstances is a giving of life. Why should that be a swear word? That's really an interesting question. It tells us a lot about the pathology of the dominator culture.) But the artist's obsession with rebellion and with the link of violence and sex is a tremendous prescription for maintaining a dominator society on a mythopoetic, subconscious level.

We're talking now about the invisible foundations of a system that everybody agrees is unpleasant at best, possibly at this point suicidal for the planet. I'm saying, let's look at what keeps it going, and the artist, unfortunately — especially so much of this deconstructionist art — keeps the system going. David, I would love you to contribute to this conversation. . . .

David Loye: I feel the people who are trying to bring about change, if forced to, must use violence. We think of the Minoan Cretans as a tremendously peaceful people, without fortifications. In fact, they had the strongest navy of their time, and Cretan craftspeople made the best swords. The reason they didn't have fortifications was that they didn't have trouble internally, because they had a society that did not generate conflict. But the only way they were able to maintain that society was to keep the mainland people at bay with that navy.

Riane Eisler: If I may interrupt, this is self-defense in a dominator world, and that's not what we were talking about. We were talking about revolutionary violence as an instrument of social transformation, and I think it's very limited.

David Loye: Let's say there are two types of violence, violence for self-defense and violence for revolutionary advance. Violence is very clearly justified in self-defense, and I see no two ways about it. Certainly, if you want to take the stance of Jesus, of Martin Luther King, of Gandhi, and say, "I will not raise a finger against them even if they tromp me," that's fine for a visionary statement, an inspirational statement. It's not fine for the bulk of people who find themselves in that kind of situation because they've got to defend themselves, otherwise what they represent and what they believe in are absolutely going to get squashed by the dominators in this world.

I think the use of violence in a revolutionary context has to be questioned very severely. My feeling is that there are situations where it can be ultimately needed but that it's something to be avoided as much as you can because history shows that it triggers massive violent retaliation. Whatever you represent is squashed, and you're perpetuating the tradition of violence as a solution.

But when I read your book, Riane, I was not only enjoying it and being excited by it, but I was also thinking in the back of my mind that there are individual people and groups of people in this world who would do anything in their power to suppress it. Within a democratic setup they're going to allow it to proliferate for a certain amount of time as long as it's isolated amongst the intelligentsia and certain ineffectual classes because it actually supports the idea of democracy that doesn't really exist. But if this ideology reaches the lower classes then it's a real threat, and the haves are not going to watch their banking empires go down without a fight. Their view is that they belong where they are and nobody else is going to mess with them. So I'm saying that the inevitable result of revolutionary ideas is conflict. Unless I'm totally misunderstanding everything being said, this is a threat to power of the most fundamental kind, so it's going to be met with various forms of opposition.

Riane Eisler: Ridicule and trivializing are the first. We're in the midst of a virulent period of dominator regression right now.

It's been mounting since the 1960s, when things were shaken up. You see it in the proliferation of pornography that links sex and death and violence and domination. That's fundamental. You see it very clearly in the dynamics of power.

Yet, in the corporate empires, something fundamental has changed more than in the political sphere. Sure, a lot of it is rhetoric about teamwork and nurturant management, but some of it is real, because the fact is that top-down, fear-based, and basically violence-backed management (I mean, the threat of firing is a form of violence — you're going to starve) is not all that productive. It certainly inhibits creativity when people are frightened. They may thrash around and produce a lot of images, but how creative are they? So there are the technological changes that we're seeing, the big shift from industrial to postindustrial society, and that's an opportunity for a fundamental social shift, from a dominator to partnership society. The agrarian revolution was prehistoric. Then came the industrial revolution. And now you have another period of tremendous technological upheaval. Again, I can't make predictions, but I know that manufacturing is shrinking, just as agriculture once radically shrank, and that different types of education, socialization, and ways of looking at what is productive for the planet are beginning to emerge — with great difficulty, but they are beginning to emerge.

So on the one hand you've got this tremendous dominator resistance that's violent in many places. It doesn't really matter whether it's a communist or a capitalist regime, because communism really turned into state capitalism; there was no real socialism — there were hierarchies and elites. So it doesn't matter that much whether it's state capitalism or corporate capitalism; neither is going to make it.

In my work, I don't distinguish between the economic and political on one side and the family and the personal on the other. What I'm trying to say is that it's very strange that even in some of the centers of power there are some of the partnership seeds for reasons that have absolutely nothing to do with making things better for humanity, but simply have something to do with productivity and creativity and the marketplace. It's not hopeless at this point, because we are in this period of incredible technological change. The industrial revolution loosened things; capitalism and communism came out of it. And I hope that maybe gylany and the partnership ideology can gain their strength out of this similar and even greater technological upheaval.

Do you see a society without conflict?

Riane Eisler: I think conflict is fundamental. It's part of the human condition. But the dominator model is a confrontational model, a model of violent conflict resolution. The issue is not conflict, the issue is violent confrontation. I think it is very important that we acknowledge that there is conflict and that there are conflicting interests. Then I would go on to agree to some extent with David that within those conflicts and interests, it's interesting how we can very often find areas of commonality. And today the issue of survival has become the area of commonality which is going to make for some very strange bedmates.

ART: DECONSTRUCTION AND RECONSTRUCTION

Riane Eisler: I'd really like to get back to the artist because some of the people who will be reading this are artists. The stereotype of the artist is of the young man rebelling — at least that has been the contemporary vision of the artist. Poor old

Michelangelo or da Vinci might have wanted to rebel, but the only way that they ever got anything at all was by pleasing their patrons. They were told, "You paint this ceiling." They may have thought, "I don't want to paint this ceiling, and I certainly don't want to put your theme up there, but what choice do I have?" With the loosening of the command system in art, you do have the artist rebelling. So instead of painting whatever they're told on the ceiling, artists are now doing something in the toilet or something like that out of rebellion.

But has the artist really done anything much? Goya *did* it. I mean, if you want deconstructionist art, if you want art that exposes and deconstructs the dominator model, look at Goya. If you want art that shows the dominator psyche, then look at Hieronymus Bosch: the dominator psyche is all there. You have Dadaism, which was nihilism, and so is most of what artists are doing today. As in music, they keep swearing instead of asking why.

Given the fact that those artists that you mention come from an earlier age or generation and really are unknown to the American masses, do you think we're experiencing a popularization here of something that Europe has already done?

Riane Eisler: Maybe punk is America's Dada. It may be a culture lag to some extent, but I don't think of America as that backward. There was an exhibit in Beirut of Moslem art, and what was it? It was blood; it was guts being spilled; it was weapons. So it is not just American art. Instead of challenging violence and brutality, instead of showing constructive alternatives, we idealize violent rebellion. Goya didn't. Goya was one of the very few who managed to show dominator violence without idealizing it. That Moslem art was idealizing it. A lot of

American art idealizes it, and I submit to you it is not coincidental that Dadaism was contemporary with so-called radical (but actually profoundly reactionary) manifestos which were viciously contemptuous of women, viciously hating of woman, manifestos of death to women, death to the feminine.

The Futurist Manifesto of the early 1900s . . .

Riane Eisler: I'm convinced that this is not coincidental, that it's basically the dominator system again recycling itself. So the artist under the guise of revolution perpetuates his —and I say *his* — own misery.

But what about an artist like Karen Finley?

Riane Eisler: I would say that Karen Finley is taking deconstructionism to a level where it has not been, and I would say that that's important. But a lot of the stuff that's still coming out is the same old stuff recycled. It's been recycled now for an awfully long time. At a certain point deconstructionism becomes trite; it is a lot of noise for nothing because it has already been said. I'm not saying that we shouldn't have deconstructionism; I'm saying it needs to go much deeper. I'm glad you brought up Finley because she's a very good example of going deeper. But I'm also saying that we need to look at reconstruction, to look at constructive alternatives, at art, to provide new visions, not a Pollyanna vision, not a never-never land. A lot of the art that's coming out of the New Age movement is nice, but it's like poster art. It doesn't really go to anything fundamental. But look at Judy Chicago's art. Now that's a different story. That's reconstructionist art. It's not never-never land, it's not make-believe. It is reclaiming sexuality, it is reclaiming birthgiving — legitimate subjects, essential subjects for art. So I'm not saying that there is no place for deconstructionism, but let's go deeper into it, and let's also move toward reconstruction.

David Loye: What I see is this: There are four different kinds of artists. There are two kinds who serve to maintain the system, whatever the system is, and we now know that for five thousand years it's been the dominator system. There are those who paint conventional things, landscapes and so on, art that isn't threatening anything, and they reassure everybody that everything is beautiful, this is the way life is. This art excludes all the people in the ghetto, and it's "nice." Then there is the art that serves the system by protesting and by raising hell. This serves the system as what you might call sandbox art. The sandbox strategy for the system is — and you see this also in social science — that as long as you can keep them jabbering down here, playing like kids in a sandbox, where they can't touch the reality, that's fine; that's the kind of stuff we can tolerate. If you look at the system as a circle, these two types are within that circle, but along the periphery of the system are two other kinds of artists: the deconstructionists and the reconstructionists, and they're the ones who are criticizing the system. The deconstructionists are trying to pull it apart, and so are the reconstructionists, but they're also trying to put it together again in a new way. By now there's enough of the pulling apart. What is so desperately needed is the reconstructionist, who has the new vision that we're hooking into.

The need will continue for deconstructionist art, since to create anything new you have to destroy old rules and relationships. The deconstructionists do have a function, but the bulk of them have been hung up so much in it that they're now part of the dominator system. They've been co-opted and they're serving as the sideshow at this time.

When it comes to visionary art, I think of Orozco. He was an incredibly powerful artist. He was a communist. The alternative that he was trying to present was the communist society, and he had pictures of bloated capitalists and police thugs and piglike generals and so on, and Christianity being co-opted by dead saints. But he was also visionary. What he was expressing was actually a movement toward partnership. The point about Marxism now is that it's old, it's antiquated; it's an earlier stage. What is so desperately needed now are reconstructionist artists, whether they're in art, in music, or in writing, who see this partnership alternative, the gylanic alternative. We need artists who are driven to express the true, the good, and the beautiful, and who refuse to be co-opted.

But to a certain extent it has been very difficult for artists to be connected to what's really happening. The world is hard. Hard places create hard people, create hard lives. People want experience. They want to see that you know what you're talking about — I know I do. When I hear New Age music, it's not that it isn't pretty, it's that I don't believe it's real. It's an escape. It's not confronting what's really happening. What you're saying is true. I think a lot of people that I know are striving to create that reality somehow, particularly women artists, as a matter of fact. All the really vital stuff has kind of a dark edge to it, which is the only thing that's believable.

Riane Eisler: Now we're talking about vitality in art and the dark edges. We were earlier talking about the link of sex and death. I'm going to free-associate a little bit with this, because I think that a lot of what animates art and gives it vitality is a connection with the basics. What is basic, really? It's birth, it's sex, it's death. That's interesting, because we have an art where birth is taboo. That rule is being broken a little bit, but in a sanitized way, like putting Annie Leibovitz's picture of a nude, pregnant Demi Moore on the cover of *Vanity Fair*. For most of recorded history the image of the naked, pregnant female body was taboo. That seems strange, once you think about it. But it fits with the dominator model's devaluation of woman and of her creative sexual power. Instead, we have death and sex constantly linked. Now as I look back on the earlier iconography, the more partnership-oriented art of prehistory, there's a link between all three, and birth and sex rather than death are stressed. But it's the missing of birth that makes it extremely difficult for us to have real art, something that's connected with reality, with the vital importance of sex, of woman, of birth. This is very fundamental. I don't know how else to put it.

Do you think that's because art is male-dominated? Because men don't have anything to do with birth?

Riane Eisler: No, I think it's because art is largely an expression of the society in which it is created. And, as we were discussing, even the rebelliousness of art, the nihilism, maintains the dominator system. (When you have nihilism, you're saying there's no hope for anything else, no hope for change. What more profoundly conservative statement can you get than that?) I am loath to say that birth is missing because men don't have anything to do with it. Men don't physically give birth, but every male is born. Every male experiences birth. So it's not sufficient to say that. It's because most of what is labeled "important" art comes from men of a certain ideology that devalues, conceals, and basically falsifies the importance of birth — men socialized in that ideology that links sex and death rather than showing the complete picture, which of course includes birth and links sex with pleasure and life.

I would say that the reintegration of birth images into contemporary art is extremely important. Because what does the artist use to create? The artist uses myths, images. And the resurfacing of birthing images reconnects us with partnership-oriented myths and realities. What is creativity? Creativity is a stimulus, and it's a process, and it's a high. I know that from writing. It's connecting with a higher mind — not necessarily in the sense that there's something out there, but that there's a region of yourself or of the universe that one is somehow connected with and comes through you, so to speak.

The muse.

Riane Eisler: Yes, the muse. And of course this [pointing to David] is my muse and he happens to be a man, which is the partnership model. Because you know in the dominator model, you have very stereotypical roles. The men are the artists, the writers, and musicians, and the women are the inspiration, the muse. In the partnership model, you are both muses and creative people, which is what has given so much vitality to our relationship.

So number one is the excision of the vital element of birth, of sexual love, as legitimate subjects for "serious" art. But there's something else in the old art, and again I'm free-associating with you. In the old iconography, death and sex are also associated, but they're associated in a very different way. It isn't the power to kill that is associated with sexuality, it is rather that you die, then there is some kind of a sexual thing that happens, and you are reborn. Do you see the difference?

Are you speaking now in terms of prehistoric times?

Riane Eisler: Yes. If you look at the prehistoric Mediterranean burials in the Cyclades, for example, people are buried in round holes, sometimes caves, with a small opening. As a matter of fact, Newgrange in Ireland is the same shape. It's a womb, with a vaginal opening. Why is that, and why are the dead facing east? It's the direction of the rising sun — rebirth. It's a different combination of fundamental elements. It's still death and sex, only sex leads to rebirth. The vitality can be there, but it doesn't have to be a morbid thing, out of control, with something demonic.

Today's artistic impulse not to be controlled is very healthy. But I don't think that the impulse to break free of the controls necessarily has to be equated with being out of control — which is what happens when you are surrounded by imagery that says no transformation, no positive resolution, is possible. The only possible thing that you can hope for then is being out of control, is going to the outer limits — even if it destroys you, even if it consumes you — and romanticizing and idealizing the destruction not only of others, but of yourself. And this is where we come back to what is so central, so critical. For I think that authentic art is an art that can express the human yearning that we all have. It's not a yearning to be disconnected, alienated, out of control, or connected with a sick dominator culture, but a yearning for connection with that which is healthy in ourselves, with our authentic feelings for an authentic vision of what the world is about. It's a vision that again reconnects birth, sex, and death in a way that is not so vile.

David Loye: This culture stresses sex and death, which comprise a very limited part of the human spectrum. The implications are that we screw around and die and that's all there is to life. It doesn't have any profound meaning, let's just get by as best we can. By leaving out birth, you leave out the cyclical reconnection, the feeling that is the basis of spirituality. This is why all religions and all spirituality have wrestled with the question of an afterlife. If you leave out birth, that reminder that we came out of mystery and we go into mystery, we're just these screwing robots here. The dominator system can only operate as long as that attitude is prevalent. The minute you've got somebody like Jesus entering it, reminding us of our humility, saying we're part of something bigger, which birth brings back, then you've got the inevitable destruction of the dominator system. But instead, we've got this bit about the Virgin Birth. Here birth does have some emphasis in one area of the dominator culture, but it's a virgin birth. In other words, it's a sexless birth, a completely unrealistic, illusionary birth. It's the perfect example of the slop and the screwing up of the mind that the dominator system sells and must have if it's to maintain its domination.

Riane Eisler: But it's much more than that, and it ties in with many of the so-called pro-life people who are really very anti-life. What you accomplish with the delinking of sex and birth and the linking of sex and death is that you take the woman out of the picture as a real carnal human being. And basically you take the man out of it too. What you accomplish is that the emphasis is on woman as a container rather than as a sexual energy source. That's the complete opposite of the ancient religion. It was a celebration of women's sexual energy.

So in one sense I would say that what Madonna is doing, as kooky and commercialized as it is, is in some ways fundamental reconstructionist work. This woman is really doing some fascinating things because she's saying, Look, I have sexual power, I'm not just a baby container or, alternately, a collection of body parts for men to get a charge out of. I am the Goddess, the feminine energy, the primal energy. The Goddess was sexual. She gave birth. She took death back and rebirthed it. Her worship was an acknowledgment of woman as alive, not as just a functional thing to plug in. That was central to the old religion, and that's a very strong image. So if it survives, you have to corrupt it, right? So what does the church do? It takes away her creative sexuality. She is just a baby container.

It's not accidental today, with this whole anti-abortion movement and the whole emphasis on women just as a baby containers, that we have a time when images like Judy Chicago's art are appearing. And it isn't just Chicago. A lot of the art of antiquity, celebrating woman's creative sexual power, seems to be resurfacing.

We're talking about what I'm writing about now. I've been very much involved in looking at what life is all about, what art is all about, what religion is all about. Art and religion deal with the same things; they have vitality. So what do these antipleasure, antipartnership people do? They again falsify. Woman becomes a container for an unborn fetus. Life is not important, what's important is this unformed organism in the womb. Once it's born, "Don't bother me with this child!" "I should give them milk money? Don't be silly." But, oh, we're going to idealize the unborn, the otherworldly. You see, it ties in with the dominator model, with the dehumanization of woman, the desexualization of birth. And it leaves intact the desexualization of life and the erotization of domination and death.

The artist now can begin to free herself or himself from this insane falsification. But so many artists don't. Some rap group yells "fuck you" or "I'm gonna to cut your cunt, baby," these horrible images of violence against women. My god, it's so ironic to have black men who are so very much at the losing end of the dominator model perpetuate the dehumanization of one human being by another, when that is exactly the model for their own oppression and dehumanization. That's a vivid example of how the artist has become enmeshed in the dominator mythos.

You can say we need imagination. But whose imagination? So much of what passes for radical art and music today is profoundly reactionary dominator stuff. That's why the imagery from prehistoric art, and the decoding of that imagery, is so important. Not because we want simply to adopt it, but because what it does is break the spell. It breaks a spell that we've all been cast under, that it is normal to associate sex and death, that it is normal to have no images of women giving birth in either secular or religious art.

Art can break the spell, the control, the mind control. I think of these young people who are piercing their poor bodies. I feel sorry for them because it is a mutilation that is being done out of a desire to experience freedom, yet it's again part of ritually becoming prisoners of a dominator way of thinking and feeling, where pain and death are idealized.

These very same people who have so much passion that they're willing to hurt themselves in order to feel are the ones who could use their vitality to change both art and society. They can see that they're into a repetitive rite of angst, that really nothing much is accomplished, that when you're out of control in that negative, self-punitive way, you're actually being controlled, because it's either the sandbox syndrome that David talks about or it's again a falsification, an enmeshment in something that offers no hope. These very same people who had the passion to go through that are the ones whom, I hope, we can now expect to come out on the other side and begin really to reconstruct, having deconstructed so much. They have the pieces now, everything is in pieces. It's like a jigsaw puzzle, and the pieces can now be shaped a different way and be put together in a different picture. You have to take the pieces apart, but to *keep* taking the pieces apart gets you nowhere. The function of the artist is to reshape the pieces, which is what we're talking about: how to remythologize art, and with it our everyday experiences, our society, and our lives. And of course some of this is already beginning to happen, not only among avant-garde artists and musicians, but also with some very well-known musicians such as Sting, Peter Gabriel, and Sinéad O'Connor.

There's a phrase that keeps going through my head, which is the artist as strange attractor, the gylanic artist as strange attractor. The gylanic artist as strange attractor is a challenge. Now that really requires going far deeper, and I don't mean sitting down and reading every book that was ever written. I mean a lot of processing in terms of using those templates of the dominator and partnership models and trying to figure out just what's what.

What does it mean when one says that to be real art has to have a dark side, it has to have a hard edge? I would say that that's only one reality. That is the reality of our pain, and that's very true. But there is another reality, and that is a chalice reality. Now for the artist to authenticate that requires a tremendous amount of deprocessing. It isn't just saying, "I'm going to paint something that offers hope."

Nobody believes it.

Riane Eisler: Not even the artist.

What we're talking about is ecstatic art as a possibility for the future. But you can't simply produce ecstatic art. Ecstatic art comes out of a true sense of connection. The yearning for connection is deep. There's a tremendous hunger for it.

I would like to challenge the artists today, young and old, to disengage from this notion that the only reality is what makes us hone our pain, because there is another reality that eventually has to become socially and ideologically and mythologically rooted, a reality that helps us hone our joy and our sense of connection and of love. That is the most abused word: love. It's a throwaway word in a dominator culture. But we need to reclaim words like *love* and *joy* in a real way.

I'm a very intense person so I have experienced both very deep despair and very great joy; the artistic temperament is that way. But for a long time in my life I was really hooked on this whole cycle of just being caught in the melodrama of the pain of my script as a woman. I almost died before I was forty because that was the only interesting script for a woman. And it's still true, isn't it? We've got the tragic heroine and the tragic hero. But I'm saying we can have an adventure in art and in life without having to suffer constantly to authenticate that all this suffering and relating to one another in a dominator/dominated mode is the "real" human experience.

The artist's responsibility at this time is to open up other possibilities, to recognize that great art is art that inspires, that not only helps us deconstruct reality, but reconstruct reality. That, however, can't be done in quick half-hour fixes for a fifteen-minute success. It requires long-range thinking. It means reaching deep inside, to really sing, to mythologize the gylanic possibility, and here is where what we are now learning from our prehistory, and from what so many of us are striving for and experimenting with in terms of real partnership relations in all aspects of our lives, can provide enormously important and exciting material.

Constructive Anger

Riane Eisler: We started off by talking about the angry young men and how, when that anger is expressed through rebellion, it fuels an illusion of change. What's really happened is just a changing of the guard, whether the sons are taking their fathers' places in the family or in the state or internationally. You still have strongmen, rule by anger, by force, by fear.

I don't want to imply that I think that anger is necessarily a negative emotion. In fact, I think that anger is a very natural reaction to an inherently miserable system. But the way the system handles that anger is to diffuse and deflect it, first of all, against powerless groups, against women, children, and minorities, then against "enemies" in aggressive wars, and ultimately in repetitive rebellion, which never touches the basic problem, which is that this is a dominator system founded on rankings, beginning with the ranking of half of humanity over the other, and going on from there. In the vernacular that is so popular today, it is a "lose-lose" system.

The dominated are obviously psychologically, physically, and economically exploited and abused. But even the dominators are always tense and uneasy, and this is really why this whole thing is such a charade. Get to be the dominator by being an angry young man only to find out that now you've got to watch out for all the other angry young men coming down the road, be it in the corporation, in the artistic establishment, in academia, in politics, or in the bedroom! (Besides that, whether you're heterosexual or homosexual, the dominator system poisons the possibility of feeling truly connected to another human being. And, of course, sexuality is a connection — not just a physical connection but an emotional, even spiritual one, in the best of cases. But in dominator sexuality you're taught to equate sexuality with domination or submission. That is not a way of really being connected, by having one person dominated and the other one dominating.) So I think whether you're alienated, as in the middle and upper classes in capitalist society, or whether you are among the people upon whose backs it rests

— and of course a lot of the economy rests on the unpaid work of women — everybody's angry.

But what I want to talk about is how one can use that anger. Anger is the thing that the young men are supposed to feel. Some of the young women have in recent times been permitted to share in it, but only up to a point, and only as long as they were sort of aides-de-camp, you know, sexually and with the coffee and with the services. Then they were able to share in the anger, but never about their own condition. If a woman says, "I'm angry because I don't want to be a sexual commodity," says, "That's not sexual liberation to me, that's not real choice for me," what is the response? Remember, we were talking about the democratization of a lot of the dominator ailments, whether it's overconsumption — more people being wasteful — or what passes for sexual freedom, where not just the dominator elites but other men have access to a lot of women. Where is the real sexual freedom for women? And what sexual freedom is there anyway in mechanical, meaningless, nonconnected sexuality? Are you free if you have to inhibit so much of yourself, if you have to suppress your empathy for others?

I'm going on about this because I think it's very important, especially coming from a woman. Women have been denied anger, and their reclamation of authentic anger is a particularly important social act. That is also true for men and their authentic anger, which is not woman-bashing! I am afraid a lot of what passes for consciousness-raising in men's groups now is woman-bashing in New Age clothes.

Do you want to name names?

Riane Eisler: No, because it is more important to identify ways of thinking. I will say that a good deal of what is currently viewed as "new" is just a variation on an old theme: woman-bashing. Yes, men have a lot of problems. But it's not because, as some of these groups claim, they did not properly separate from their mothers.

The impulse to find something that is transformative is very healthy and it is part of the gylanic/partnership thrust, which I see as a movement toward health, not toward an ideal state. Who knows what that is? We're human, and not violence-free. There will be violence, but it needn't be institutionalized, systematized, glorified. But what we have in some, though by no means all, the new men's groups is the co-opting again into the dominator model of this healthy, transformative impulse. So now it's not the angry young man from the Left, it's the New Age young man screaming in the woods against his mother and his girlfriend and why are they limiting him when he's the wild man. That's not what's limiting him.

Anyway, women have a wild side too. And women are searching for a new spirituality too, to replace the spiritual betrayal by so many of the institutionalized religions, which have for most of recorded history served to reinforce and maintain a dominator society. The real betrayal of some of the New Age gurus is a betrayal of that search for a truly new spirituality.

ETHNICITY AND MORAL SENSITIVITY

With that, I'd like to pose two large questions. The first concerns nationalism. The second concerns the transformation from a prepatriarchal society into a patriarchal one — how that took place historically. When anybody has claimed to speak for humanity, be they communists, anarchists, feminists, or whatever, they are not only faced with the vast diversity of cultures and histories that make up our species, but they are also confronted by representatives of warring camps. Some of these, for example, would seek to invalidate your claims on the basis of your European ethnicity. This is particularly true in the arts which are, by their nature, expressions of particular cultures.

Riane Eisler: First of all, I don't see a contradiction, because the gylanic model — the partnership model — celebrates diversity whereas the essence of the dominator model is to equate diversity (beginning with the differences between women and men) with ranking, with either inferiority or superiority. Once you free yourself from that, then there's no contradiction between honoring diversity and at the same time saying, "Let's relink birth, sex, and death in different ways, in ways that remythologize and authenticate human experience, in ways that give value to a less brutal and more creative human experience, where sex is not dirty and death is not holy and giving birth and nurturing life are given more value than threatening and taking life." Every single culture can do this in a different way — out of its own texture, its own particular experience.

So I don't see a contradiction. I do see the fanaticism that defends dominator traditions. I also see the denial and the hypocritical pretense that what is being "protected" is ethnic diversity, when all too often it is rank and privilege and brutality.

One example is a statement quoted in a section of *The Partnership Way* concerning genital mutilation, where an African woman talks about the men in her culture in their shiny black Western shoes defending ethnic traditions that oppress women, pointing out that they obviously want to retain only those traditions that maintain their domination, that justify their brutality. So we have to look carefully at nationalism, because all too often it is just an excuse to set up ethnic, religious, or gender hierarchies all over again without dealing with any of the basics.

But when people are struggling against oppression, isn't it natural for them to seek identity with their fellow sufferers? Isn't it natural for them to bond together for protection and liberation?

David Loye: I have been looking at all this from the point of view of science and of moral sensitivity. The tendency in social science today is toward relativity, saying that all these different societies and all these different tribes have different moral codes — that's the diversity of humanity and one mustn't disturb it. But the fact remains that underlying all this diversity you have these two models — the dominator and the partnership models — operating even at the prehuman level. And at the human level you have the dominator model prevailing for over five thousand years, corrupting virtually every society on the face of the earth. So we have a situation where if we're going to reclaim our cultures, reclaim our histories, reclaim our collective or national or racial identities, we have to clean up our act. We must get rid of the dominator elements, wherever they're now entrenched. It's fine to celebrate one's ethnicity, one's national identity, but look what's happening in Europe. We're seeing the rapid rise of the old antisemitism, of racism, of nazism. You simply cannot tolerate that sort of thing in your fellows, of whatever race or ethnicity, just as you cannot hang on to female circumcision and expect any decent person to respect your cultural tradition. There is this contradiction in thinking today, but the resolution can only be in the partnership direction, given the thrust of human evolution toward higher and higher forms.

Riane Eisler: On the other hand we could be like the dinosaurs and not make it. There is certainly that possibility. This is just one little planet in a vast universe.

THE SHIFT FROM PARTNERSHIP TO DOMINATION

Let me try to connect this question with the other one I posed earlier. Much of the evidence you bring forth to support your position in *The Chalice and the Blade* is archaeological findings in the Middle East, the Mediterranean area, and so on. Many people I've spoken with have asked, "But what about Africa, what about Polynesia, pre-Columbian America?" In fact, if you had more or less stable societies going back a couple million years where humans were occupying various parts of the globe and living in nonpatriarchal societies, why did patriarchy happen? Where did the barbarians come from and how did they actually manage to spread throughout the globe?

Riane Eisler: It didn't happen simultaneously. But let me start at the beginning. The key elements of the configuration that I call the dominator model are strongman rule (be it in the family or the state), rigid male dominance, and a high degree of institutionalized violence. And as you move toward the partnership model, you get a more equal gender partnership, a more truly democratic society. Such a society doesn't require that fear and force be institutionalized and idealized in order to keep the system together, because there are other bonds, bonds based more on linking rather than rigid ranking.

Both of these types of social organization are possibilities for us as a species, but you have to look at the whole configuration, the whole picture, which has not been the way we have been taught history, anthropology, archaeology, or anything else. Prehistory was not part of the picture. Women were not part of the picture. So it was not seen that a more equitable distribution of wealth goes with a decrease in male dominance, it goes with a greater emphasis on nonviolent conflict resolution, and so on. In addition, scholars were strapped (as many still are) into a nineteenth-century evolutionary stages model, with history inevitably moving from lower to higher stages. My model of history is not like that. It's interesting how every one of the philosophical systems, Marxism, certainly Freudianism, has a story of how it all happened. The Marxists' story is very much in line with the nineteenth-century linear stages of upward progress. Mine is not a linear upward model of cultural evolution, which the evidence simply does not support. I think that both the dominator and the partnership models probably go way back into our protohistory, that those types of societies developed very, very early. Where did the Kurgans, the hordes that overran the prehistoric civilization of Old Europe, come from? They had to come from somewhere, and they already had a dominator social organization.

There are various speculations as to how this all worked itself out. My own belief is that it's entirely possible that in the very beginning of our emergence as a species you had both groups orienting primarily to the partnership or the dominator model. But you certainly do when you get to about 5,000, 4,000 B.C., when you first begin to see the appearance of massive dislocations in the more peaceful Goddess-worshipping agrarian societies of the Neolithic, when you begin to see the displacement of these societies by warlike, male-dominant hordes.

Viewed in terms of chaos theory, what we see here is a bifurcation. But we have to consider what happened to trigger the Kurgan invasions. There's a geographer by the name of

James DeMeo who has studied this intensively. (DeMeo is particularly interesting because he is a Reichian. I think Reich sort of had it and didn't have it; he had a lot of the pieces, but he got diverted into sexual repression as the problem rather then looking at sex in the context of gender.) DeMeo found that there were massive prehistoric climate changes, tremendous droughts, with consequently horrible social dislocation, scarcity of the worst kind. And this is when we also find mass invasions and a general shift toward the dominator model.

You said that you think it's probably a conflict that is deeply rooted in antiquity, way back in prehistory. If there was a point in time, say a million years ago, when humankind had spread out from eastern Africa and was pretty much all over a good portion of the globe but in very small tribal groupings, would you say that some of those would be partnership model societies or would they be evenly divided into dominator and partnership models?

Riane Eisler: No, not evenly. Let me make that point very clear. I think that in those areas that were fit for human habitation there was much more of a chance of getting a partnership-model society. Given human sexuality, which is very much oriented toward the pleasure bond, given the long child-rearing period, which requires cooperation, bonding, and partnership for survival, given the fact that humans seek to avoid pain and find pleasure and that the dominator model institutionalizes pain, chances are that the mainstream of human development probably flowed more in a partnership direction. But what happened was a reversal. What used to be a fringe phenomenon in less hospitable areas, which was the development of dominator social organization, then became mainstream.

That's what I believe. I don't have proof for it a million years ago. I have a lot of data indicating that this actually, factually, was the case about five thousand years ago.

I understand. The reason I asked, the reason I put it in that kind of a context, is simply because the question arises about paradigm shifts and their very nature. What makes a paradigm shift happen? Chaos theory explains it in a subatomic way, which can be extrapolated on a sociological level, but how it actually happens is a historical question, not quantum mechanics.

David Loye: Let me put this in the context of a very important point about chaos theory. What you find, for example, in *Order Out of Chaos* by Ilya Prigogine and Isabelle Stenger, is the viewpoint of natural science, or of mathematics. But when you apply this study of patterns to living humans, you move from natural science to social science, and this is a hell of a big change. Riane's book is extremely important within this movement because it is an application of chaos theory and systems science to cultural evolution.

Now let's see how this works, because I think this sketch may answer several questions you raise. At first you have what Riane outlines in her book. There is this earlier period of the predominance of the gylanic or partnership ethos over much of the globe. It tends to occur wherever you have an economy of abundance, in the fertile areas, for instance. But out along the periphery there is a nomadic culture, where they're living off a flock of moving animals. Now the question keeps coming up as to where these nomadic peoples, the Kurgans, came from, and more importantly, how did they become such rotten bastards. As the work of Jim DeMeo shows, tremendous climatic change had much to do with it. The steppes of Russia, where many of them came from, are still subject to vast changes in climate. So you have these people who probably started out in the wet centuries as peaceable types saying, "It's going to be good here forever. We're going to be able to grow a lot of stuff, so let's settle down." But then year by year the drought spreads, until at last they're forced to become roaming nomads, and now in the ways that chaos theory and systems science help us understand, we can see how the dominator model that forever after guides them is built bit by bit.

Now in order to survive, to have something to eat, they are killing a lot of animals from their herds every day. Their life depends on killing. But these aren't just the occasional unknown wild animals they killed much earlier in the woods. These are now animals with whom they have developed a special relationship. They have protected, fed, and lived closely with these animals. Their children have pets among these animals and many of the young sheep, pigs, and so on may have been given affectionate names, as we do with Porky Pig or Bugs Bunny in the cartoons. Now they must harden themselves, kill this meaningful thing, rip off its skin, chop it up and eat it, so that they have to become callous, brutalized by this experience. And now these roaming tribes are beginning to bump up against each other, fighting over scarce grazing land. Inevitably somebody discovers that it isn't just animals we can kill. In the same way, we can kill people and take over their territory. Now when you've got a system like this developing, the next step is for the biggest, toughest, strongest guys to rise to the top. And next is the tribe that can build the most vicious weapons.

This is not just speculation on my part. This is what archaeologists have found in the drought-ridden steppes out of which the Kurgans emerged. Here, working upward layer by layer, archaeologists have found artifacts supporting this interpretation until they reach the layers in which weapons of a new order of destructive capacity appear. There is nothing else in the world at this early point in time to compare with the sophisticated weapons of these nomads, soon to become world-class marauders. Archaeologists have dug up scores of carved stone monuments to their gods and chieftains that show figures of warriors who are absolutely plastered all over chest and belly with battle-axes, spears, arrows, swords, and daggers. And this is not only a display of the advanced state of their weaponry; it's also a display of what they value most, the instruments of killing. So they're valuing killing. They're worshiping the power of the strongman. They've got the hierarchy. And then, next step, these lovely people discover that they can tame horses.

Now they've got the perfect battle weapon. They can ride down on defenseless people who don't know anything about horses, and it's just like a bunch of nazis in a panzer tank rolling into a grade-school playground. They tromp all over everybody in their area, getting practice for the big move, and the next step is obvious.

As the climate gets even worse, and their population is bursting at the seams, they look over there to the west, where the peaceful Goddess-worshipping cultures lie, and they say, "Hey, those soft people over there have a lot of food and goods. They've got a lot of pretty women and everything else we want. So why don't we just go over there and lop them off and take over?" So they start moving westward. They become the "peripheral invaders" and the "strange attractors" of chaos and dynamics theory, and in a relatively short period of time, just a few thousand years, it's over and we're saddled with the dominator model and the dominator ethos for five thousand years.

That didn't precipitate the change everywhere, did it?

Riane Eisler: The climate changes seem to have been the trigger.

David Loye: It was happening in many places, probably with slightly different patterns leading to the same result.

Riane Eisler: But I think that we have to be careful not to say the cause was just climate, that this is only environmental determinism or technological determinism. So let's get the broad outline. What certainly seems to have triggered this was something like the kind of chain reaction David describes. But even more importantly, we begin to see another dynamic: what happens when the dominator model and the use of force are institutionalized. Everything begins to change, and you would find that within communities that were not decimated or taken over there would probably be fundamental changes. You see the traces of that even in Crete. For example, if you take the whole spectrum, from the early Minoan to the middle Minoan to the late Minoan and then the Mycenaean culture in Crete, there are no signs of armed invasion there, but there's an increased militarism. Why? Because there's a narrowing ring, a constant, intensifying threat from the outside, and the internal structure changes.

I think that you really have to see these changes in terms of systems transformation; it wasn't just brute force invading, but also something from within. I think that's very important. In a sense that's a hopeful thing, because if some of the means for the transformation from a more partnership-oriented to a dominator social organization were internal dynamics, that had a great deal to do with remything, with changing the mythology as well as the social structure. It was not just a question of bashing people on the head. Then we can see that today again remything has a great role in changing social structure. Then we know that we can reverse that process without reinstitutionalizing force. And we're back to the question of the inefficiency of force, because force after all was the catalyst that brought this on and that then became institutionalized in a "more civilized" way under law, custom, religion, and mythos.

PARADIGM SHIFTS AND THEIR TEXTS

But what do you see in the present situation, which you've already described as a very regressive period, that indicates a paradigm shift is even possible in the foreseeable future?

Riane Eisler: I see a lot of indications. There is tremendous strengthening in what are, in the language of chaos theory, strange attractors rather than the static attractor of the dominator model. There are, in Prigogine's language, many small nucleations of partnership all over the place. There are couples working on relationships where there is real sharing of parenting and household chores, and getting away from the male and the female roles, to be just two human beings (though the burden today is still primarily on the woman in most cases). It is a tremendously important point that these are even issues that people are dealing with, that women and men are working for egalitarian relations. So also is it that so many people are talking about a dysfunctional family based on control. (Of course, that's a dominator family, and people are trying to get out of that, trying to come out of denial.)

I'm purposely talking about the personal now because without changes in our personal relations we are back to the same dominator dynamics under different names. Changes in personal relations are the most important partnership signals; they are the core of the new nucleations. But it has to be at all levels. During the last decades people have been pouring into the streets asking for everything: peace, disarmament, women's rights, an end to repressive rulers in the Soviet Union, and so on. These are all important partnership movement signs. We've also seen the ecology movement, the changing consciousness about man's conquest of nature — recognizing that's dominator stuff that isn't going to work. These are all very real, tangible indications that a paradigm shift is possible. And we see these signs even in the corporation, where they are talking about teamwork and nurturant management styles. These are all still little blips, and they're still on the periphery of the system, but they are there.

Cultural transformation theory does offer a framework for all of these nucleations. The comment that I hear from people most often is that it shows how things fit, including my own experiences and my own life. Now if we don't see how these various seemingly random things fit together, okay, then we don't have a new paradigm.

But how much does it hinge on having the book, whether it's the Bible or _The Chalice and the Blade_?

Riane Eisler: It doesn't hinge on that. Of course, social movements have very often had a book. There are many people who are now writing their books using the terms _gylany_ and _partnership_. But one book I think, in this age, will not the trick do.

Unlike the _Communist Manifesto_, unlike _Das Kapital_?

David Loye: I think the main thing one realizes about this partnership idea is that, from one way of looking at it, all Riane has done is simply pin down what is going on more forcefully than anybody else that I know of. She's describing something that's already under way, that's been in motion since the time of the Enlightenment, and she's putting it into context as a whole. But one of the world's best-known anthropologists, Ashley Montagu, didn't call Riane's book the most important since Darwin's *Origin of Species* out of some idle impulse. He said that about this book out of his profound scholarship and understanding of how things fit together. This is a remarkable new picture of twenty-five thousand years of human cultural evolution. I think it is the kind of watershed book that Rachel Carson's *Silent Spring* was in relation to the ecology movement, or Helen Caldicott's books in relation to the peace movement. You can find certain other books playing this role in relation to the feminist movement, but I think in relation to getting across the nature of the challenge we face — survival of our species and all other life on this planet — her book is pivotal, and it will be recognized as such more and more over the years.

Actually, the reason I asked that was precisely because of that Montagu quote on the book's cover. I'm sure the publisher needed to call everybody's attention to that. But that's exactly my point, that it's not a question of flattery or anything like that. The issue is, can ideas actually have that kind of power? Because we were talking about movements and social forces. You were talking about the tangible evidence of forces for change and I think that is so important, particularly in the context of a really anti-intellectual environment. The actual level of discourse is so low it's embarrassing. So in that context, a lot of people, particularly young people, have really lost any confidence that an idea can actually motivate anyone. All that matters is bitches and money, as the song says. You don't motivate people with a powerful idea. That's sort of resigned to the past. Christianity or communism or some other failed movement just proved that it's no good to follow anybody.

David Loye: May I just mention something else about this book? The books with great historical impact do not have to be profound. Harriet Beecher Stowe's *Uncle Tom's Cabin* had a hell of a lot to do with the Civil War because, in part, it was a mass readership book, it reached millions of people. But it was not a profound book. The point was that it rang the bell, it caused a mighty resonance at a specific time in history. And that's what's happened with Riane's book. It's hit at the resonance point. Darwin's *Origin of Species* was not a book for the masses. But *The Chalice* is interesting because not only is it profound, it also reaches both the elite and the mass.

Riane Eisler: Well, some of the mass. It may reach a lot of nonacademics, but it hardly reaches the mass.

That's actually another reason I asked, because, for example, although our magazine, *Komotion International Live & Kicking*, has a very small readership, it's an important readership that you won't otherwise get. That's the point. I think there are ways to access certain constituencies that are otherwise completely isolated because the world's been cut up into little categories and niches, and to read a book is almost to put yourself in another category. You talk about some of these subjects and it turns people off. This is true even among artists, because for them it's "live fast, die young, and leave a good-looking corpse" and that's it. And that's the mythos.

Riane Eisler: Well, it's the rock-group mythos.

It goes along with the whole death culture. Let's face it, everybody wants instant change.

Riane Eisler: It's the half-hour television program.

Exactly. If you're not a hit tomorrow, it's not worth doing, so the contradiction gets flipped upside-down. Instead of always making the attempt and persevering, because it can matter, you say it didn't happen right now so it doesn't matter, or it can't matter.

Riane Eisler: Let me tell you something that is very important in terms of the artist. Whether the artist likes it or not she or he is marketing ideas through imagery, through music, through words. And for the artist to say that the idea does not matter displays ignorance about what art really does. Art supports or challenges certain ideas. Art introduces new ideas, and ideas are not devoid of emotional charge. I do not think that feelings and ideas are two separate realms.

The artist can make an idea numinous by investing it with a tremendous amount of emotion, a tremendous amount of charge. I'm told very often about my book, that yes, it has a lot of scholarship and a lot of data, but that it also has passion and spirituality. That is the artistic part of it. And that is the part that made it numinous in some degree. So first of all, I would say that for the artist to negate the importance of ideas ignores the history of the role of the artist in maintaining and changing culture. I would also say that people who have been brought up in an electronic-media era have a difficult time with this concept. But you can't ignore history. Books have changed cultures. Ideas have changed cultures.

I do hope that my book can provide an alternative for people. Capitalism and communism, return to old-time religion, addiction —what are the alternatives? There is a field that is barren; it's littered with corpses. This is an idea struggling to emerge. I've articulated a lot of it in *The Chalice and the Blade*, but when I say that the important thing now is for other people to take it, I think that's part of the partnership model; it is more pluralistic. Yes, I think that if we do move toward a partnership future, my book will certainly have a place in history, but it will be accompanied by many more. I don't see it as a monolithic event. Does that make sense?

Yes, it makes a lot of sense.

ANARCHISM AND PARTNERSHIP

David Loye: The subject of anarchism relates to one of the dimensions we're talking about here, and perhaps the takeoff point is the angry young man. The angry young man or woman comes along, seeking his or her way intellectually, and at some point encounters, whether knowing that it's anarchism or not, a view that says let's get rid of government and just relate as individuals. A central doctrine of at least one branch of anarchism is that there is natural goodness in human beings. So the idea is that if you just get the rotten institutions out of the way and relate as good people together, it'll all work out somehow. This has a long tradition. It actually goes back to Zeno of Citium, the Stoic philosopher of the third century B.C. In modern times it comes up again in Proudhon, who was one of the social utopians engaged in the argument with Marx and Engels about how to organize society.

Then with Bakunin the idea of using violence to seize power entered anarchism. So you began to have this situation in anarchism where the angry young people took sides between those advocating violence and those against it. In this country, of course, somebody identified as an anarchist killed President William McKinley, which in turn killed off anarchism in the U.S. as the backlash against this social philosophy escalated. If people dared to deviate from established thinking, the authorities labeled them anarchists. Anarchism was what communism became later as far as a label to justify witchhunts was concerned. The famous Sacco-Vanzetti executions took place in such a climate of backlash and fear. A factor at that time was the disagreement between the anarchists and the Marxists. The great figures were the wonderful Peter Kropotkin in Russia and the wonderful Emma Goldman in the U.S. Their books are just plain tremendous, as fresh and meaningful today as when they were originally written.

In more recent times this conflict over whether social action should be violent or nonviolent has surfaced in the youth movements. Particularly in the student riots of 1968 here and in France, you find this pattern in which an idealistic movement gets under way with leaders who are nonviolent. Soon, however, the advocates of violence move into leadership. They frequently come from unsatisfactory homes and often have a tremendous storehouse of rage against one or the other or both parents that merges with their rage against the unfairness and the inequities of the prevailing system. This can be so powerful as to push them entirely out of anarchism into nihilism, where the idea is to tear it all down, to tear down all the existing structure and start over again. Well, what all this accomplishes, over and over again, is what happened in this country after the killing of President McKinley. It leads to a dominator regression — to the backlash which strengthens the dominator system. It is one of the great tragedies of anarchism in this century that the social-psychological dynamics that go with it set off this cycle and thus the dominator system becomes more entrenched.

The same thing, in another way, happened with communism. The Bolsheviks were the violent ones; they not only vanquished anarchists like Kropotkin, Goldman, and Makhno in Russia, but also over time stamped out the better side of communism. Ultimately, this helped lead to the Cold War and the locking of these two massive systems, the capitalist bloc and the communist bloc, into a self-perpetuating death dance of Mutual Assured Destruction. This result radically escalated the challenge of finding better ways of carrying out revolutions, ways by which you're not building up this tremendous backlash every time. We'll never get out of the dominator system, we'll never escape it, as long as we continually build up this backlash. The great social psychologist Kurt Lewin — whose work in this regard I explain in my book *The Healing of a Nation*—found that we must use ingenious ways to lower the dominator resistance. We must outsmart it, get around it, and so change the mass consciousness that in the end we can simply shove aside the dominator consciousness and system.

This is what's beginning to happen, I feel, with the partnership movement. It's too early to tell whether it's going to accomplish what is needed. The feminist revolution is accomplishing a great deal, as we can see in the election year of 1992. But the partnership movement has this added ingredient of offering a way of defusing the male orientation to the male power structure — of undermining this age-old alliance, of lowering resistance to equality for women and thereby equality for all. You say "feminism" and many men (who are captives of the dominator system) tighten up. You say "equality" and they tighten up. But you say "partnership" and suddenly they begin to open up. This is really what they want, they realize — and they're ready to shift allegiance from the male dominator power structure to a partnership structure for humanity.

Let me ask you a couple of questions because you've made a number of loaded comments. I'd like to go back to the beginning when you mentioned Proudhon. Not long after Proudhon and Marx began fighting it out in the ideological trenches, so to speak, workers in the streets were taking control of the city of Paris. The Commune was ultimately defeated by force; you might call it the dominator backlash. But that didn't stop the revolutionary movement. On the other hand, it did set the stage for the preeminence of Marxism over anarchism. *The Poverty of Philosophy* by Marx won out over *The Philosophy of Poverty* by Proudhon. I happen to agree with Marx in his more radical socialism. But Proudhon's mutualism was not typical of all anarchist thought. Kropotkin called for anarcho-communism; he tried to reconcile the dispute by concentrating on the goal of total change you're talking about. What I'm asking is why anarchism did not prevail. Here are these ideas that are being put forward by Kropotkin, Goldman, even by revolutionaries in Russia. How did they lose if their ideas were better?

David Loye: I think they lost because the Bolsheviks were more tightly organized and ruthless and authoritarian. This was in keeping with Marx's original faulting of the social utopians, including Proudhon. In effect he said, "This is fantasy! These people aren't going anywhere because they have no effective way of hooking into the system and really changing it. Nobody's going to pay attention to this. It's great to get together in small groups and praise each other and dream, but it's not going to change anything." So the Bolsheviks just marched in and took over.

But is what you're saying about the anarchists true historically? Were the anarchists incapable of organizing mass movements? Were they incapable of delivering the goods? Or were they in fact infected themselves, as you were saying? Wasn't your point that from within their own movement there were these two tendencies which actually weakened their ability? Isn't that the key historical question? We know that they lost. The anarchists did not take power anywhere except in parts of Spain. So in terms of social revolution the question is, did anarchism fail because of confusion over violence as a strategy? Because it didn't stay true to the ideas that Goldman, Kropotkin, and others put forward? Up to this point, anyway! There are many people out there who will say that anarchism has not failed yet.

David Loye: Frankly, I see anarchism as one of the precursors of the partnership movement. It's difficult to articulate, but anarchists had this kind of dream. Unfortunately, it was a male-dominant group, which opened them to the problem of becoming a mirror image of the system they sought to overturn. They had a few strong women like Emma Goldman, but even they were overshadowed by the males in context after context. I also think, as I've indicated, that a big part of the problem with anarchism was the backlash against the violence that it engendered.

I also think that this was a movement that arose at a time before history was ready for it. But it was very definitely not a failure in the way that history works itself out with social movements. Everything seems to fail eventually, but the useful thoughts and the meaningful experiences are sources for the future. Seemingly little things may have existed for only five years, let us say, but they can have an impact on the future, like rivulets or creeks that flow into a river. Of course, what we're all hoping is that we're swimming in a creek or river that's going to lead us to the ocean.

Riane Eisler: Also, in a dominator model of society, anarchism often becomes libertarianism; we've seen that. It becomes a basically self-centered, insensitive individualism. And it becomes a struggle to see who is "stronger."

Do you mean individualism versus the state?

Riane Eisler: That's right. You get Ayn Rand's exaltation of unbridled individualism in *The Fountainhead*; that kind of thing. So that's one variation of what happens in a dominator model. Another variation is that it becomes violent, with violence built into its very ethos. That was the basic problem with anarchism, and the reason it got such a bad name. But it is not inherent in anarchism, which I would define at its core as a way of structuring economics in a participatory and somewhat decentralized way. I say somewhat, because if you look at the Basque cooperative, Mondragon, there is also central planning there. But it is not a top-down command structure, and there are various units. It isn't like capitalism, where you have these giant corporations gobbling up more and more formerly autonomous units.

But for that kind of anarchistic, nonhierarchical, and truly participatory economic and political democracy to work, you must have the missing ingredient, which is where the partnership systems model comes in. How can you talk about a truly participatory society if women are not fully included? So even Mondragon will not last unless something is done about the social foundations, unless attention is paid to whether we relate in a democratic and participatory way in our intimate relations, in our gender relations, our sexual relations, our family relations.

Communism, the attempt to realize the socialist vision, failed in the Soviet Union. This was not only because it did not allow enough participation by both women and men and thus wasn't really communism (in fact what you got in the Soviet Union was state capitalism). It was basically because it didn't have the necessary foundations. It became another dominator system because people never had the chance to learn patterns of economic and political democracy in their day-to-day relations, particularly their intimate relations in the home.

We know that women worked far longer hours in the Soviet Union than did men, that it was very male dominant. That's clear today, and so is the fact that there was a lot of violence in the Soviet family — not that this is only the case for the former Soviet Union. In every society where violence against women and children is condoned, there is this basic model for violence by the powerful as a means of establishing and maintaining control. So you're not going to get these gentler relationships and these more equitable relationships in the economic arena or the political arena unless you have the foundations for them. And that's again where the partnership movement comes in.

A lot of the components of what we're trying to construct, which is an integrated partnership model, have emerged historically much earlier. But because there was no integration, they have got lost again. What we need is an integrated partnership movement. And we're right back to the angry young man and to sex and to death, because the dominator model can only keep going through the socialization of men to dominate, to control, and to conquer. Whether you've got an anarchist or socialist or capitalist framework, you still have that fundamental problem, that the caretaking work — the nonviolent conflict-resolution, even the feeding, that basic nurturing work — is devalued because it is relegated to women.

Also, who cleans up the mess?

Riane Eisler: Precisely. It is relegated to women; it's despised as women's work. So you're not likely to see the funding priorities for a clean environment. Or for "soft" welfare-type programs, programs for feeding people, for caring for people. You see what we have all over the world. So, while I think we owe a great deal to all progressive philosophical and political movements, we need to look at them very carefully and unravel and reweave them into new patterns. We need to leave the dominator threads behind as best we can, and to reweave old and new threads into a partnership pattern.

My partnership vision, then, certainly incorporates the more caretaking philosophy of socialism, be it idealistic socialism or scientific socialism or communism, as well as the idea of seventeenth-century liberalism that people have certain inalienable or fundamental rights. It also incorporates the feminist idea that not only men but also women have these inalienable rights. Then it adds to this a systems approach, the analysis of society in terms of two very different alternatives, the dominator and partnership social and ideological configurations.

And certainly the vision of anarchism, which is one of cooperative, participatory, more decentralized, and more effective units fits into the partnership model. So does the fact that many corporations today are dismantling, internally, into smaller units where people work in teams for commonly agreed-on goals. You could call that an anarchic concept, couldn't you?

In a sense, except that you have the problem of ownership.

Riane Eisler: Well, that's the issue and that's where a cooperative like Mondragon, which is owned in a participatory way, comes in. But, in any case, if we don't pay attention to the basics, to male and female socialization, to what happens in homes between women and men, between parents and children, none of these things can be implemented. Because you still have a basic model for structures that oppress and exploit people. And let me add that we also need to pay attention to our mythology, which at present idealizes conquest, domination, and exploitation.

SEX, CONNECTEDNESS, AND NURTURANCE

David Loye: Every time I get involved in a discussion about the partnership approach, I try to put myself in the skin of a social activist out there in the audience or readership — a social activist who may be feeling very frustrated because while she or he is hearing a lot of concepts and a lot of talk that's appealing, it's hard to retain any sure sense of what it's all about. In other words, if I came in cold on a discussion of the partnership approach with my interest in social activism and in changing this world for the better, I would feel impelled to demand that you give me one thing, one set of actions that I could consistently pursue that would lead me toward this better world. One of the great strengths of Marxism was that Marx and Engels were the first to set forth a specific set of steps for activists to take in relation to a comprehensive theory of social action. Marx was saying over and over again, Follow these specific steps, which will pay off according to this theory, and you will get there.

Let me suggest that, although much more needs to be done, if we do nothing beyond building the movement toward gender equity, equality of the sexes, getting more women in politics, more women in leadership, in business, and greater respect and equality for women in the home — if we do only this, we will see far-reaching effects in all spheres of society. If you look at this process in systems terms, what this will mean through the interlinkings and interactions this type of action will generate at every level—psychological, political, economic, spiritual—throughout the whole social system, you can see that there will be a vast reduction in tension and conflict through the transcendence of the pathological dynamics of the dominator-dominated relationship. There will be a vast reduction in wife beating, child abuse, incest, wars, insanity, rape, murder, and violence of every kind.

You would also see a vast change in our attitudes toward sex. There are connections between sex, spirituality, and the equality of the sexes. Get away from what are essentially sadomasochistic relations in dominator sex, and you get a tremendously liberating, life-enhancing relationship. I found that, hidden in his private notebooks, Darwin observed that what becomes moral sensitivity in the human is evolutionarily rooted in the development of sex far back in time. More and more complex kinds of animals evolved over millions of years, and there is an evolutionary track which leads from the development of sex to the first faint sign of parental love in the reptiles, to the first sign of sociability at the next higher level, to finally what Darwin called the moral sense in humans. Now this would just seem like so much philosophical speculation except that a brain researcher, Paul MacLean, in a work that has been virtually ignored for thirty years, concluded that this has been the sequence in the evolution of the brain. In fact, I'm collapsing Darwin and MacLean together in the sequence I've just described. MacLean found that there is in effect a "neural ladder" going from the sex level in the limbic system of the brain to the areas in the frontal brain lobes that we definitely know are associated with moral sensitivity. This suggests to me that the subject of sex is central to the question of how the partnership revolution is to be effective.

How do you define sex? The sex act? There's certainly plenty of sex out there.

David Loye: This is sex as the drive for linking, for bonding, and for caring.

So you would say that in our society it is simply diverted? I see sex everywhere, and there's no caring, no bonding at all.

David Loye: This is sex in its deepest meaning. In other words, within this view that we are descended from lower organisms and that we represent a flowering of evolution, there is this drive throughout evolution toward bonding, toward linking up. Organisms bond together, they link up, and this comes from the original sex drive. This is what draws us to one another. Of course you can divert sex, you can degrade it. You can also eat yourself silly. Any of the other drives can be taken to an extreme or diverted into other channels.

Riane Eisler: As I said earlier, the book that I'm finishing now deals with human sexuality — not animal sexuality, because it's very different. We're a very different species. We have needs and capacities other animals do not have. It is true that through dominator socialization we have learned to eroticize domination and violence as sexuality. For example, it is not accidental that in periods of growing partnership movement such as ours, you get in response this barrage of images relinking domination and violence with sexuality.

I think what David is talking about is that we humans have an enormous yearning for connection. And human sexuality, which is very different from the sexuality of most species, is part of this. But this yearning for connection is not only sexual. There is also in humans a survival need for connection as infants, for touch, for caring touch. We express this yearning in many ways, including spirituality, which is often described as a feeling of oneness, of connection, with what we call the divine. I don't think we can separate those things. But that's exactly what's been done in dominator religions.

But how do you define connection? It seems a bit ambiguous.

David Loye: One way connection can be defined is with the idea of sympathy. In other words, I feel your pain, I feel your distress, I feel your pleasure, I respond to you. The secret to dominator control and the secret to the dominator tragedy, which is our tragedy, is disconnection. Males are taught from day 1 or day 1000 to disconnect. They are taught to be tough. They are taught not to be sympathetic. Or they're allowed a certain amount of feeling within a limited range, like within their own family. But you are taught as a male — and the teaching becomes ever more strict the higher you go in the power structure — that you cannot advance unless you disconnect. You cannot fire people, you cannot order people into war, you cannot exploit people. You cannot do all these things that are associated with the dominator system unless you have disconnected, unless you cannot feel the other's distress. And that's the secret of the dominator system, of the male tragedy, which the system forces upon us as males, and it also forces upon females who are put in a position where they have to act like males.

Riane Eisler: We were talking about practical things to do, and what I see very vividly now is that we're moving to a new kind of politics. It's a politics where empathy is an issue and intimate relations are an issue. Take the issue of sexual harassment. It has become a political issue, debated in public. Notice that a lot of the dominator types don't want it to be a political issue. In fact, they say it's not fit to be talked about in public.

Why? For good reason. Because the moment we talk about these things in public, some collective action can be taken to right the power imbalances that are inherent in matters such as sexual harassment. So I think that from a practical standpoint we are at the threshold, or in the very baby-step stages, of a new politics no longer only dealing with power relations at the top of the dominator pyramid.

We began the modern movement toward partnership by focusing on power imbalances. It began with a challenge to despotic monarchs, right? We wanted to have a more representative, more democratic kind of government. We didn't achieve it. But the ideal was articulated. It's the same thing with economic democracy. Now we're moving toward dealing with the foundations. It's very interesting. Issues like violence against women and children are becoming more and more a part of the international public discourse.

Several years ago I wrote an article for *The Human Rights Quarterly* called "Human Rights: Toward an Integrated Theory of Action." It is reprinted in *The Partnership Way* and what it basically says is that you can't split off women's rights from human rights and get human rights for anybody. Since then I've written another piece called "The Human Rights of Women, Children and Men," bringing in the parent/child dimension that is so critical.

Now we are seeing international conferences focusing on women's rights as human rights. I am very involved in one such conference taking place in 1993 in Coeur d'Alene, Idaho. I am very excited about that because 1993 is the United Nations Year of Human Rights. In the official U.N. conference in June there will probably be just a little bit about the human rights of women and children, a little appendage to themes such as the torture of political prisoners. But why *wouldn't* these men enjoy torturing political prisoners (and they obviously enjoy it), if they have been socialized to associate acts of torture, acts of violence, acts of terrible cruelty and even killing, with sexual arousal?

As we begin to deal with those issues in the public sphere, we move toward a far more realistic model of what politics is about. Because politics is about power, about who holds power and how it is held. Today we're trying to move from a dominator politics to a partnership politics. That was the idea of economic democracy, political democracy. Now we're talking about those concepts where they begin, where we rehearse and practice them every day, in our intimate relations.

Some critics of your thesis seem to oversimplify it into a male versus female choice. Obviously, you go to some length to spell out the gylanic concept, but it might be fair to ask you if you see any potential danger arising from an imbalance toward the feminine nurturance direction comparable to, if different from, the dangers that the present masculine dominator imbalance entails.

Riane Eisler: First of all, I don't think maleness and femaleness have much of anything to do with this.

Do you mean biologically?

Riane Eisler: Biologically. Absolutely nothing, as far as I'm concerned. What has a lot to do with this are the social constructs that we call masculinity and femininity. And how masculinity and femininity are constructed is very, very different in a partnership or a dominator model of society. Let me focus on this one thing. If you had a true partnership family, both mothers and fathers would be nurturant, which is what a lot of people are trying to move toward.

We all know that when we talk about nurturing we're talking about the kinds of things that mothers traditionally do—and I don't mean only changing diapers. I mean caring for a child when the child is ill, touching, hugging, feeding the child. Mothering kinds of behaviors are nurturing behaviors. The reason that I said it's not maleness and femaleness is that if we really do have a partnership family—and this is the fundamental point—then male identity no longer needs to be defined by a boy or man as distancing himself from the empathic nurturant behaviors, because in such families both mothers and fathers can do the nurturing, as so many men are beginning to do today. So I hope this issue of masculine and feminine that we're dealing with — and there's a lot of stuff out now about reclaiming the feminine for men, and women accessing their masculine, and all of that — is a transitional phase. Because all that we're trying to access and reclaim is a certain part of our human repertoire as *both* women and men. I really want to be very clear on that. When a man is nurturing, he is only feminine as defined by dominator stereotypes. In actuality, he is accessing not his "feminine" side but his full humanity.

Now, getting to the question you posed, I cannot imagine a global society where there is a danger if we have too much caring and too much empathy. What is too much empathy? What is too much caring? If caring is really the norm globally — for the whole family of nations — then I don't see a danger. On the contrary, I can see a society where people are far more creative. Countless studies on creativity show that many very creative men have come out of families with nurturant mothers; it's quite interesting. And I'm sure women are also more creative when that capacity is nurtured in them. I know that from my own experience living with David, who has been very nurturant of my creativity. Nurturing does encourage creativity. So I don't see a danger in nurturant behaviors — nonviolent conflict-resolution models — be they between different races or different nations. Or between women and men. Or between men and men — as long as that is the global norm.

There's always this idea put forward that men will be too soft, that men will be "wimps." But I do not define strength as the superior ability to beat up somebody. Sure, that's a dominator definition of strength. I think people are strong if they are able to pursue goals effectively, if they're able to make a commitment to life and to other human beings effectively, if they're able to withstand the vicissitudes and problems of life that we'd have regardless of whether we are in a partnership or in a dominator society. There are storms, there's sickness, there's death. There are always challenges to our strength. We wouldn't have perfect human relations, even in a world governed by a more stereotypically "feminine" ethos.

GETTING FROM HERE TO PARTNERSHIP

OK, but there are likely to be roadblocks on the path from here to there. In response to those, people — maybe unwillingly, maybe unwittingly — may end up opting for the leader who pays lip service to good goals but says we have to fight for them, we have to kill for them, and eventually the end will justify the means.

David Loye: How do you explain Gorbachev? Gorbachev was in for only a certain amount of time, but he was a man of peace who led the world away from the brink of nuclear war.

He gave up power nonviolently, but he's out of it.

David Loye: So is Abraham Lincoln. Lincoln was out of it because he was shot. There have been other leaders displaced;

that's the nature of leadership. Your point of course is, in a sense, what is the effect of these people when they are continually swallowed by the dominator system? What is happening today in the way of a developing strength for the partnership ethos is shown in the case of Gorbachev. I'm convinced he was the first major leader fully to realize the significance of the hydrogen bomb. And the mass consciousness has picked up on it. There has been a growth in both leadership and mass intelligence because we're beginning to recognize that we could be nearing the end of evolution. We're seeing that our species could wipe itself out. What happens to you if you have a heart attack and you realize you face death? You reprioritize everything in your life. I think the same thing is happening to humanity at the level where people can begin to think beyond how to get hold of a few grains of rice to survive the day. There is a growth in this mass intelligence that is intimidating and pushing back the dominator ethos.

But does that adequately answer the problem when, for example, in my neighborhood there is an increase in violence? In my alternative occupation three cabdrivers were killed in two months. I go out on the street every night and it's much worse, and not only is it much worse but the way people react to it is absolutely animalistic.

I'm driving my cab. I pick up a black person. He gets in and the first thing he says is, "Thank you, it's hard to get a cab!" and I know what he's talking about. The whole thing that comes out in that one interchange is survival, what survival means on the street. To me as a cabdriver it means I discriminate on the basis of instantaneous stereotypes, and it's pure animalistic behavior. I didn't have to justify it to my ride. I said, I'm not a social worker. I'm out here making a living. I don't owe you anything. You get in the cab, I take you where you want to go, you pay me the money. If I feel like I'm threatened, I'm not going to take you. You didn't threaten me. That's all. On the other hand, as a human being I understand your predicament. In fact, I share it! You're a person trying to get home from work, and cabdrivers see you come out with dreadlocks and kind of wild looking. They're probably scared of you.

But I told him that both of us are trapped, and I explained that my position is that I judge people on behavior, how as individuals they act, and I'm not always right. I've been attacked. I'm lucky to be alive, as a matter of fact, but I reject judgment on the basis of race or any other superficial stereotype, because it's ineffective. However, most people do make such judgments; that's simply how it is.

So here we are sitting in a cab, shaking hands at the end of the ride, and I'm telling you that's where the world has gotten, not to the other side. Do you understand what I'm saying? People in his position and my position would frequently look at your position and say, "You're not there, man! That's okay if you've already got it, but when you're out on the street and you don't have it, it's fuck it — the hell with the system, I don't want any part of it, destroy it all."

David Loye: Exactly. And this was predictable twenty years ago. In fact, in *The Healing of a Nation*, which I wrote back then, I did predict it. I believe it was clear then that there would be terrible consequences if there was not a change of national policy on the racial front, where everybody — black, yellow, brown, red, whatever, and white — felt excluded from the system and hopeless. For the past twenty years the young have been a major factor in this free-floating, nihilistic rage. The young feel there's no future, that the country's going to hell.

Langston Hughes wrote that wonderful poem about a deferred dream. Does it dry up, he asked, like a raisin in the sun? That's what's happened in this country, that's why you have the explosions, because there's no feeling of inclusion. All these people have felt exploited and have felt that there's no hope. They feel there's nothing out there and it's not going to get better. For twenty-five years, enduring Nixon, Reagan, and Bush, they've been offered no leadership that speaks to their needs and aspirations.

This is a much more powerful impediment to social movements and social progress than simple brute force is. There are many obstacles facing any social movement, but the internal defense mechanism that prevents people from daring to dream, daring to commit to anything bigger than their immediate survival, is one of the most difficult obstacles to overcome. This is why it's so important to emphasize that beneath all the rage, both directed against others and directed against ourselves, evolution has given to all of us an innate drive toward goodness, and it's in there punching away, persisting year after year. It gets stepped on. It gets crushed. But it keeps coming back.

The thing that excites me now, that sets off our time from any other time in human history that we know of, is that it's becoming evident we face extinction of the species unless we get intelligent in a hurry. I think there's a lot of evidence that people around the world are getting the message and they know the old dominator consciousness has got to go.

It seems from your answers that two things are going on. One is that attempts at social transformation get crushed because the haves don't want the have-nots to have; that's pure and simple. But on the other hand, within the oppositional movements themselves there are deep conflicts that lead to their defeat.

David Loye: Let me give you the example of the partnership movement, and how in this new movement we're having to deal with what all other movements have had to deal with. The people who are drawn to the partnership movement, every last one of them, including Riane and me, are people who have been hurt and maimed by the dominator system. There's a hell of a lot of pain in all of us because of what we've suffered. What I see in the partnership movement are all these people, many of whom have read Riane's book and got from it this dream of a better world. They get together in groups and often there is all this rage and pain that have got to come out. There's this fear that the dream isn't going to come true. They have all this cynicism that protects them. There's this fear to dare to dream. And when you get in the presence of the dream it reminds you of how awful things have been. What then happens, time and time again, ties into these dynamics we're talking about.

There are certain people within the partnership movement who take leadership. They are good people, highly intelligent, and they try to provide the structure for the others. They raise questions about what the group should be doing, and so forth. In some groups this works fine, but in other groups they become focal points for all this rage and animosity that needs to get out. They become, in psychological terms, the victims of a transference. They become the focal point for all the animosity toward the mother or the father or whoever hurt the hurting person in the past.

Closely akin to this, there also moves in some groups the need to have no structure at all. We will have no elite, they say. No, we're all going to run this thing together because nobody is better than anybody else and so on. So they chop down their own leadership, they become a formless, unhappy sprawl. People come to these meetings and say, "To heck with this. These people can't even get their act together; how do they expect to transform the world?" "You know," they say, "I'll go play pool or what the hell, I'm not going to join a group where the people don't know who they are to begin with, and they all sit around jawing about it." So we see there has to be a process for working out the pain going on simultaneously with learning how to develop leadership, to encourage leadership, this leadership that has to learn how to empower others rather than say you do this, you do that. In many ways, we see in the partnership movement the same challenges, the same dynamics, the same problems that every movement previously has faced. Only this time we hope to solve the problems by getting to their roots in terms of a new gender-holistic understanding of what gave us these problems over thousands of years, and what can get us out of them.

I'm glad you're getting into this because this answer takes us into some really important areas both in terms of questions that people raise and of previous experience with revolutionary movements and revolutionary struggle. It was characteristic of the Marxists to be better organized, to be more efficient. Look at the history of it — the Bolshevik revolution, the Chinese revolution — nearly half of humanity under two very powerful organizations which, initially anyway, changed property ownership for the first time in thousands of years. They were the only people for ten thousand years who got it out of the hands of the capitalists and the feudal lords and put it in somebody else's hands. The same people had been owning everything since as far back as history went: the same families, everybody passing it on down. So this is persuasive evidence to support their claims. Meanwhile, the anarchists and other utopians are unable to get effectively organized. Hell, I'm a musician, and getting a band of five people together is hard enough! But perhaps by examining some of the mechanisms by which the anarchists were defeated — how movements that are not, in the main, violent, seem to be defeated all the time — we could get somewhere. How do people who want to get away from the cynicism and despair and into the struggle deal with that problem?

David Loye: We have to learn how to organize and work together in a mutually respectful setting, developing and accepting the right kind of leadership, encouraging the group, and identifying with it, rather than atomizing into individual power struggles. That's the thrust of the partnership movement, in contrast to many other ways.

To pose the threat the other way: the rightists fall in line. There is no problem with organizing there. Phyllis Schlafly or Jerry Falwell or Ronald Reagan says something and they all fall in line. There is the authoritarian model. It's not hard to organize if you have that. "I'm a follower, I follow the leader; the leader speaks, I follow and I don't rock the boat. I don't speak up unless I'm called upon." Much of our educational system is designed to produce exactly that type of person.

On the other hand, there are more advanced people who feel the idealistic pull toward a better future more profoundly, who have learned to be independent and stand up for what they believe in, but who have a hell of a time organizing. The challenge that faces us is how to create the situation and the settings that help these people learn the organizational skills for group power.

How does the partnership vision transform the actual character of an organization or institution?

David Loye: A starting point is equality for the sexes. That's the fundamental lever of change, the fundamental revolutionary intervention mechanism.

But how will that affect institutions? Organizational structures? One of the things that has interested me about Michel Foucault, whether you agree with him or not, is his examination of the mechanics of how systems work to maintain power relations. It's not that people necessarily buy into the ideal, it's just the fact that that's the way the system works. It's like a machine that seems completely impartial and completely devoid of content, but actually it embodies the power and the power itself is reinvigorated by the way the machinery works. So we inherit the machinery, not just the bad guys. How much of the structure has to change? How do the institutions themselves carry the dominator system within them?

Riane Eisler: I think that structure is crucial to what we're talking about. We cannot really function in a partnership way within dominator structures. They won't permit it. Where the emphasis has been on trying to change the structure of the political system and even of the economic system, I return to the basics, to woman-man and parent-child relations and to the structure of the family.

But I want to add something. There's always been this argument, especially after Marxism, that it's only the material conditions that count and that consciousness follows the material conditions. I don't look at it that way. Being a systems person, I look at it as an interactive process. Obviously, Marxism changed a lot of structures and that process began with a change in consciousness. But it didn't change them enough, because Marxism was not partnership-oriented enough; it did not offer an integrated partnership model.

As the failed policies of Lenin show, abolishing the family — having no structure — doesn't work. One of the things that Kurt

Lewin found was that in unstructured situations, the dominator model would inevitably take hold. Why? Because there was a vacuum. So our task is not just to dismantle existing structures, as the stress in revolutionary movements has been. Our task is to replace them with partnership structures.

And our task is to begin with the foundations, which are the relations between women and men and parents and children. If we are to build a partnership society we have to start with partnership families. The United Nations Year of the Family is 1994, and the basic issue for that year is what kind of family do we want to strengthen. If we strengthen dominator families, we'll have a dominator society. If we strengthen partnership families, we can build the foundations for a partnership society.

How can you strengthen something that doesn't exist?

Riane Eisler: But partnership families *are* beginning to emerge in bits and pieces. In those families where both women and men are sharing more in the housework, sharing more in the childcare, you are altering the structure of the family. That's only one type of partnership family. That's a heterosexual one. I don't know where it will go, but there will be a multiplicity of family structures in a partnership society. The point is that there will be new structures.

Another kind of family is obviously a homosexual union. We have the heterosexual and we have the homosexual. Except for unequal homosexual relations — for example, the Japanese samurai warrior castes encouraged relations between older men and young boys, just like the Greeks, where the young boy was basically taking the subordinate role of the despised woman — except for that kind of relationship, homosexuality is a real threat to the dominator model for three reasons. One is of course that lesbian relations offer women an out from male dominance in the dominator heterosexual family. The second is that for men to take the "feminine role" — that is, if it is a partnership relationship between two consenting male adults, not unequals — threatens the whole concept of masculinity as being one of domination. That's why straight dominator guys get so horribly uncomfortable at the mere mention of homosexuality, because it threatens their notion of what it means to be a man. Also, calling sensitive or more empathic boys and men "queers" is still another way of maintaining the dominator norm of "masculinity" as toughness and insensitivity. And third, homosexuality is a threat because the dominator model is one of conformity. So you impose one kind of family — a procreation-oriented, male-dominant, authoritarian family as the only kind of family. As in the 1992 Republican convention "family values" rhetoric, that's it. There is no other kind of family possibility.

I think this would be a good time to interject a question that you've provoked. In calling for the abolition of the family, which is in the *Communist Manifesto*, wasn't what was being suggested the abolition of the bourgeois family — the elimination of the enslavement of the woman as the man's property?

Riane Eisler: Yes. But the problem, the tragedy, is that communism did not offer a replacement. It did not encourage, much less give social priority to, the creation of an alternative partnership family structure. So marriage is abolished — big deal. You know you can have just as much of a dominator relationship based on sexual stereotypes without getting married if you don't change the pattern of gender socialization but instead leave the stereotypical male as dominant and superior and the female as subservient and inferior. For example, there was absolutely no effort whatsoever to get men to share in the homemaking. There was some talk about socializing housework. It got no place. Though there was some child care, really changing child care into a partnership between women and men was not even discussed. Changing the politics of housework, and with it women's double job burden, was not discussed. Changing the design of relations, the social architecture, wasn't discussed. If you don't change the infrastructure, if you don't provide for an alternative structure — this is exactly the point you were making, isn't it? — you are talking about these ideas, and nothing more. The socialist experiment did not give priority to changing those structures. Quite the contrary. Look at what happened to Alexandra Kollontai. She understood a lot about the relationship between the dominator model in intimate relations and the dominator model in political relations. And they practically massacred that woman in the Communist Party — ridiculed her; Lenin, everybody. So where was the support for an alternative structure? There was a lot of rhetoric, but it didn't happen.

Don't you have to destroy the structure itself, because it is so stamped with the domination tradition?

Riane Eisler: I am not arguing about that. For several centuries now we've been seeing the deconstruction of the dominator family in bits and pieces. What do you think the high divorce rate is about? What do you think single-parent families are about? What do you think the increasing openness of homosexual unions is about? What do you think the commune movement was about? It was about both deconstructing the dominator family and experimenting with some structural alternatives. But — and this is really fundamental — the society doesn't give support to those kinds of families.

If a group of older people say they want to be an intentional family because it's more emotionally supportive and economically feasible for them to do this, where are the tax benefits? Where are the insurance breaks? Where is the social support for that kind of family? Where is the child care for the two people who work, so they can both go to a job, so they can be with their children part of the time? Why isn't there on-site child care? We're struggling with these issues now. We are now beginning to struggle with changing the structures. Why did the Bush administration keep vetoing unpaid parental leave? You have to ask yourself why unpaid leave is a threat to American business. It's not a threat to American business. On the contrary, those countries that have it — which are most of the industrial democracies — often have higher productivity and less absenteeism than the U.S. But it *is* a threat to the dominator model.

So a lot of these things that in our time are becoming political issues are really about changing the structures within which we have been trapped in our personal, intimate relations.

But I want to stress something. I'm emphasizing the family as a foundation. Obviously the same kind of changes have to take place in all the institutions — the workplace, for example. The interesting thing is that even within the capitalist production context, we're seeing some movement toward a different structure. One might say it only serves to perpetuate an oppressive system. But the point is that in every aspect of social life people are confronting the absurdities and contradictions of the dominator model. Where teamwork and cooperation replace robotic repetition of tasks, productivity goes up.

In government, the welfare state has gotten a bad name. Why should welfare have a bad name? Because it's caretaking behavior — it's a more nurturing "feminine" role for the state. Whereas the traditional dominator view is that all the state (being run by men) should be doing is the stereotypically "masculine" thing: to defend against other states.

And to police the masses.

Riane Eisler: And to police the masses. Because in a rigid dominator society the function of the state is also to maintain rigid rankings, to put people in prison or to execute them if they challenge these rankings. In other words, to punish, and to punish violently. That's a dominator definition of the state. Frankly, there's nothing wrong with the state. This may alarm some people because so much political and economic theory has identified the state as the culprit. But this simply mystifies what is clearly a social construct. In that sense I really dissociate myself from anarchism. Because we do need government, which is of course where the state is needed.

The good thing about anarchism is what we talked about earlier — the more decentralized cooperative cluster or complex. Again, Mondragon is a good example of that because it's a complex of cooperatives. Many cooperatives fail because they don't have the banking system to support them. They don't have an insurance system to support them. There's just a factory or a grocery store or something that can't survive by itself. But as I said earlier, even Mondragon will not last unless it adds to that institutional infrastructure a partnership family or a variety of partnership family structures, which will inevitably bring with it a nonstereotypical, nondominator gender socialization—a partnership gender socialization. We're always back to the basics.

Let's get to sexuality, which is so important. I see a lot of advantages to serial monogamy as at least one of the central tendencies. There is something about having a bond with somebody, about not having one-night stands. It's just nice for most people. Everybody wants a certain amount of experimentation, but that's not what we're talking about. We're talking about a structure. For some people it may be lifelong. For some it may last as long as it lasts. But the crux for that to work in heterosexual relations is a communal responsibility for the care of children. Much of the present social disorganization is due to the fact that we don't value mothering. If our society truly valued mothering, welfare mothers would get paid for mothering, which would give value and dignity to that work, instead of just barely getting enough so that they and their kids have some food and a roof over their heads. But there is no value placed on nurturing and caretaking. That is the most absolutely lunatic thing in the world, isn't it? We are back to dominator economics. We have money for prisons, to control and punish, but we do not have money to help kids grow up not to go to jail, to nurture them. And we are back to the politics of gender, and to the higher valuation of what men and not women stereotypically do, regardless of the social costs, of the horrible costs to women, children, and also men.

Doesn't a lot of this actually come down to men taking advantage of no-fault divorce to flee their kids?

Riane Eisler: It comes down to men's living standards going up, as they still do upon divorce, and women's and children's living standards going down. There is no necessity for that to happen, by the way. But there is no interest in this from the male judiciary, the male legislature, the male law-enforcement agencies. They just aren't interested in doing anything to equalize that situation.

This is the reality, and I feel that it's very important to be realistic. Yes, we have to maintain our visions. But we have to recognize that what we are dealing with here is very long-range change. This is not a half-hour television program in which everything is resolved in a few minutes. What we're talking about is a long-range commitment to partnership.

It's also enormously important that we recognize that the dynamics I'm describing mean that the greater the partnership thrust, the greater will be the dominator resistance. This will be the case until, at a certain point, there is either breakdown or breakthrough. Especially for this readership, people already out there, already working on change, it is essential that this dynamics be understood.

And we also have to deal with violence. Violence must be demystified, not ignored or denied. It is how the dominator system maintains itself. Violence — institutionalized, structural violence — is the essence of the dominator model. So why wouldn't we see violence in reaction to attempts to replace it? And of course, it always begins and ends with violence against children and women. If we are to deal with this violence effectively, we will have to dig it up by its roots.

David Loye: Let me make a case for optimism with three points:

One, I am convinced that we are an intelligent species. This is the result of billions of years of evolution that have given us as a species an enormous intelligence that we're just barely scratching. This intelligent species has been hit with a new message which is that we face wipeout unless we get smart in a hurry. We're hit with this message by atomic bombs and by a mounting barrage of evidence from scientists and the ecology movement about what we are doing to the planet. This is one reason for optimism. When you're confronted with going down the drain, suddenly you get smart and act smart.

The second point is, as Riane's book brings out, there was this earlier time which I see as a time of greater moral sensitivity. I see it relating to an evolutionary thrust toward moral sensitivity that goes back billions of years. Now I see something comparable happening in our time, a moral resurgence that is a switch to the earlier direction but on a vastly more advanced technological plane.

The third point is how this seems to relate to chaos theory. Viewed with this theory in mind, history reveals different, nonlinear dynamics, where all of a sudden out of nowhere — out of a carpenter in Galilee and a bunch of ragtag fisherman, for example — very rapidly in historical terms, extremely rapidly in evolutionary terms, the whole system is transformed. Riane gets into this very briefly in *The Chalice and the Blade*. That is a reason for some optimism, because we are obviously involved in a time of potentially rapid systems transformation. We also face the possibility of an attempt at transformation's being damped out again, but all in all it doesn't feel to me that we are going back. We tend to get bogged down in the news of distressing dislocation, the ethnic wars, the terrible famines, the plight of the homeless. But there is, in chaos-theory terms, this configuration of the strange attractor. I think the strange attractor this time is the partnership future. It's an ancient attractor that has exerted its influence repeatedly throughout history, surfacing only for a brief time in the sun, and then it goes. It's been building up steam now for many years, and I think its time has come.

By "its time," what sort of time frame do you mean? One lifetime? Two lifetimes?

David Loye: That is a difficult question. I think it's going to take place over the next century. I think the next century will be the century of transformation.

Human evolution is now at a crossroads. Stripped to its essentials, the central human task is how to organize society to promote the survival of our species and the development of our unique potentials. In the course of this book we have seen that autocracy cannot meet this requirement because of its inbuilt emphasis on technologies of destruction, its dependence on violence for social control, and the tensions chronically engendered by the dominator-dominated human relations model upon which it is based. We have also seen that a gylanic or partnership society, symbolized by the life-sustaining and enhancing Chalice rather than the lethal Blade, offers us a viable alternative. The question is how do we get from here to there?

Biographical Conversations

RIANE EISLER

Where do we begin? Where did you begin, Riane?

Riane Eisler: I, like most people, have asked questions throughout the course of my life. My work is an attempt to answer those questions, which arise out of life experiences. In my case, I was born in Vienna and when I was a very little child everything in my world was suddenly threatened, interrupted, by what in terms of my conceptual framework I would call a massive dominator regression: the rise of the Nazis. One day I was this cute little girl in a family of some affluence and . . .

What did your parents do?

Riane Eisler: My father and mother were in the wholesale cutlery business. What happened to us was very dramatic. From one day to the next we were suddenly the enemy; we were Jews and therefore people to be hunted.

You know of *Kristallnacht*? It was called that because of all the glass, the windows in homes and synagogues broken during that pogrom, that night of terror and of violence against the Jews of Germany and Austria in November of 1938. That night some men came to our house and took away my father.

But besides that trauma of seeing my father beaten and pushed down the stairs, for me a very, very important thing happened that evening. My mother recognized one of the men as being somebody who had worked in my parents' business and to whom they had been very good. And she became furious. She said, "How dare you come here! We have been so good to you, this man has been so good to you, and now you come and . . ." She could have gotten killed; that is a risk that she took. But I don't believe she was thinking logically. She saw the man she loved being taken away. Now, the head of this raiding party — because that's what it was, yes it was Gestapo, but it was also Austrian lumpen-proletariat coming in to loot — the guy who headed this group said to her, "I cannot give him back to you because somebody else is in charge downstairs in the truck. But if you bring so and so much money to Gestapo headquarters this evening, you will get him back." And she did.

I think the authoritarian personality reacts to anger, and her rage saved our lives. I suppose it helped that my mother looked a little bit like a poster of the Aryan woman. She happened to be Jewish, but she had blond hair, blue eyes, pink complexion, the stereotype. I think that combination of rage and looking like an Aryan did it. It was very frightening, but it was also a very interesting lesson about courage. Because what saved us was not the courage to kill, but a courage born out of love, out of caring. The courage to stand up and to take a risk, not to do violence, but to speak out against injustice.

If my mother hadn't spoken out, we would all be dead. There is very little chance that we would have survived, because what would have happened would have followed a typical pattern. The Nazis took the men first, but the women and children waited. Of course the men didn't come back, and in the end the women and children were also rounded up.

So we were lucky. And we were also lucky that my father was among those who were arrested early. Because people who stayed as things got worse and worse kept hoping that the Nazi nightmare would go away. In fact, that's why a lot of "assimilated" Jews had stayed in Germany after Hitler rose to power in the early 1930s. We were assimilated Jews. I remember we had a Christmas tree. It was supposedly for Mitzi, the woman who took care of me, but really it was there because we thought we could blend. What we did not understand is that in a dominator model of society there is always the "in" group and the "out" group, and in times of real dominator regression scapegoating is inevitable. We are seeing it in the world today. Women are being scapegoated, ethnic groups are being scapegoated. That is what's happening again in Europe, and it is very dangerous. In some places it is Jews. In other places it is Moslems. Or Croatians. Or Christians. It's whoever happens to fulfill that need.

So we fled. We left at the beginning of 1939, bribing our way out. We were also lucky that we had some money. We went to Cuba because you could bribe your way into Cuba too. The Nazis had an interesting system. You couldn't get an exit visa until you had your tickets, but you couldn't get your tickets until you had an exit visa. So obviously there was bribery, which in a sense was good, because if they had all been "incorruptible" they would have killed everybody. So we went to Cuba. We were on the last ship before the *St. Louis*, which was the ship that got turned back. I don't know if you know that story.

You might relate it briefly.

Riane Eisler: A tremendous wave of antisemitism was being created in Cuba by the Nazis. On the surface, the issue of the *St. Louis* was over money. But of course the Nazis were making it a test case, to see whether their "final solution" would work. It was in June 1939. I remember standing by the waterfront, looking out at that ship, unable to understand how this could be. How could these people be turned back to an almost certain death? Every Jewish refugee on that ship had paid the Cuban government what at that time was a huge amount for a landing permit. But suddenly the Cuban government, the then president Federico Laredo Brú, decided that the landing permits were not valid. And while the Jewish Agency unsuccessfully negotiated with him (he demanded one million dollars within forty-eight hours), the *St. Louis* was ordered to sail on. It sought asylum in the United States, as it passed near the Florida coast. But the U.S. did not take it. And even after $500,000 was deposited in a Havana bank, the Cuban authorities still refused to let it land. So nobody in this hemisphere let it land. As for the U.S. —you know, "bring me your poor, your suffering masses" — forget it! They sent the people on that ship back. They were able to land in Belgium, and some were granted temporary asylum in Britain, France, and Holland, as well. But of course the war soon began, and many of them lost their lives, as we would have if we had sailed on just one ship later than the one we boarded.

We did not lose our lives. But since the Nazis had confiscated (that is, officially stolen) all we owned, we were now very poor. So I grew up with next to nothing. For the first years in Cuba we lived in circumstances that for me and for my parents were quite hard: cockroach-infested tenements. But my father and mother were very bright and they were people who didn't give up easily. My father couldn't work because Cuba had protective labor laws. Foreigners could not work. So he started his own business.

For them and for me, as for those living around us, life was an intense struggle. We lived in the industrial area of central Havana. In the tenements all around us, right next door, one could see and feel the pain, the violence. So with all this, I again had to ask myself very early on, "Does it have to be this way?"

If you remember, I referred to questions related to that one in the introduction to *The Chalice and the Blade*. Do we have to have all this violence, all this brutality and injustice? Do we have to hunt and persecute each other? Do we have to have war?

I also saw very early the "war of the sexes." As much as women and men wanted to love each other, there was this warfare in intimate relations, and the impression that made on me was as profound as any other.

How long were you in Cuba?

Riane Eisler: I was in Cuba until the end of World War II. My parents couldn't get into the U.S. I was born in Vienna, but they had been born in a part of the Austro-Hungarian empire that after World War I became Romania. Under their immigration-quota system, the U.S. let in very few people from Eastern Europe. So because what was once considered Western Europe through the vagaries of war became Eastern Europe, my parents had to wait until after the war, until their quota number finally came up. We came to the U.S. in 1946. I finished high school in Los Angeles.

The reason I asked more about Havana and when you came to the U.S. is because obviously it has a bearing.

Riane Eisler: This was not Castro's Cuba. I want to stress that. It was pre-Castro Cuba. I do want to tell you one other thing about my childhood which is quite interesting. My parents, like many Jewish families, valued learning enormously. So while they had nothing, they still somehow sent me to the best private schools. Perhaps that was one reason we never moved out of the poorer part of Havana. Another reason was that my father had by then built up a business and he wanted to be right next door to it, so we continued to live in the industrial area. In the two floors below where my parents and I lived there were about ten families per floor. But still we stayed there, even though I went to high school in the suburbs, in Vedado, to a café-society private school.

Every day for me was culture shock. Every day I took the streetcar from this very poor part of Havana to mix with these incredibly rich people. And that was very important in a way for me too, to see these polarities that there were in Laredo Brú's Cuba, Batista's Cuba, Grau San Martín's Cuba. It was very important for me to see that kind of economic injustice.

That, too, influenced your questioning.

Riane Eisler: Yes. Of course, it wasn't until many, many years later that I systematically set out to answer those questions. I made a lot of attempts to understand all that I had experienced, all that had happened, because my education certainly did not give me the answers. Most of what we are taught in school is about the dominator model of society. (Of course, I didn't look at it that way then.) But I did a lot of learning on my own. For example, when I went back to Europe in the early seventies, I went to Dachau. I wanted to see the concentration camp where we probably would have been sent to be killed. It is interesting to me that even though it was painful I didn't go into denial about the brutality in the world, I did not suppress my feelings, my empathy. Instead, I tried to understand. I became very interested in sociology and anthropology, and also in socialism and feminism and anarchism — in all of the social movements to change society. Only later on, as I began to see the underlying patterns, did I begin to understand the need to integrate those movements. But my systematic study of what I call the dominator and partnership models of society really didn't start formally until about ten years before *The Chalice and the Blade* was finished.

What was the degree you were pursuing?

Riane Eisler: Many different ones. I couldn't figure out what I wanted to do. I was in English. I was in industrial relations. And I can't remember what else. I finally graduated in anthropology and sociology. Then I went on to law school, which I quit to marry my first husband. But after ten years, after the birth of my two daughters, I went back to U.C.L.A. and I got my J.D.

Now I have to say, because we tend to think of schools and universities when we talk of learning, that some of the most important things I have learned, and continue to learn, are not from my formal education. To begin with, we are not taught to love, to care for others, not even our children, through formal education, though in recent years sex education and parenting education are beginning to appear. I have learned, and continue to learn, a great deal from my children, both from them directly and from the parent-child relationship. And of course I also have learned a great deal from David, both emotionally and intellectually, about life, about social science.

In fact, this one-to-one intensive learning outside of the conventional educational setting runs through my life. For example, my first marriage was to an engineer who knew a lot more about the physical sciences than I did. Among our very best friends in Los Angeles were some people in the history department at U.C.L.A. This was very important to my education. Talking to them, listening to them, was like having top private tutors in history — from ancient to modern.

Of course I also read an enormous amount. I was particularly interested in ancient myths and archaeology. I was always very interested in politics and economics also. And in literature and psychology. So I was already moving toward a multidisciplinary approach without knowing it. But, as I said, the formal multidisciplinary study didn't start until about ten years before the book.

I've written a lot, both fiction and nonfiction. The first of the two nonfiction books that were published was called *Dissolution*, as in divorce, and that's what it was about: no-fault divorce, marriage, and the future of women.

I discovered feminism in the late sixties. I was the attorney who incorporated one of the first women's centers in the U. S., the Los Angeles Women's Center. And I founded probably the first legal program in the United States focusing on what we would today call women's law. In those days you said "women and the law" and people said "what?" There was no such consciousness in the late sixties. I started to speak and to organize and I ended up doing a lot of family law. Another woman and I also wrote a friend-of-the-court brief to the U.S. Supreme Court, trying to convince the old men on the court (that was before the appointment of the first — and so far only — woman justice) that women should be considered persons under the equal protection clause of the Fourteenth Amendment to the U.S. Constitution. They didn't buy it in that case (*Perez* v. *Campbell*), but they bought it a year later in the *Reed* v. *Reed* case (1971). So that brief was a way of educating the court, which is what a friend-of-the-court brief does. We were arguing this revolutionary idea that women are people.

Dissolution came out of that kind of activity. I was very active. I could see what was going to happen with no-fault divorce, which was passed by an all-male California legislature, with one guy who really wanted to dump his wife of about thirty years heading the pack. I said this no-fault divorce is, in principle, a very fair and sensible law, but there's one problem with it. We don't have a very fair and sensible society. There's a tremendous power imbalance between women and men. And so I predicted (that book came out in the mid-seventies) what actually happened, what today we call the "feminization of poverty," in which formerly middle-class women and children slip into poverty.

I also wrote the only mass paperback on the Equal Rights Amendment, *The Equal Rights Handbook*. In those first two books, I used law in the way that social scientists had until then used literature, as an analytic tool. Legal writings are much more precise than other writings, and of course reflect the views of those in power, so I don't know why more people don't use that approach. If you read the laws, for example the family laws of the nineteenth century, it is not just a question of opinion that women were considered male property; it is right there, in the laws. But I was also interested in law as an instrument for social change. So I was doing work that eventually led to an examination of social patterns as matrices of the equitable or inequitable, authoritarian or nonauthoritarian, and so on. I was beginning to see in these patterns what I later called the partnership and the dominator configurations. And I want to say that I wrote *The Equal Rights Handbook* with David. Because by then we had met.

What was the fiction like?

Riane Eisler: First I wrote theater, and one of my plays was called *Infinity*. I was very much into art and technology. It was performed at the Pasadena Art Museum, later the Museum of Modern Art and now part of the Norton Simon Museum. The play was multimedia and very mythical. On the strength of that

I was invited to join the playwright unit of the Actors Studio West. I was then very interested in ritual theater, which in the sixties and early seventies was fascinating. It did get very repetitive from the mid-seventies on, but now we're finally beginning to see some really new stuff.

I also wrote short stories, but those have not been published. I could probably get them published now because of my reputation, but I'd rather finish with my cycle of nonfiction than muddy the waters with earlier work.

Just to finish the thought—you're working on another book?

Riane Eisler: Yes, two in fact. Since *The Chalice and the Blade* was published, I have contributed to many anthologies in one way or another. I also wrote the introductions for a number of books. I've published a lot of articles in scientific journals. And of course, together with David, I wrote *The Partnership Way*, an intense study and action guide that is the practical companion for *The Chalice and the Blade*. I have a contract for one book and the other one is nagging and tugging at me, but they're not the books that I announced toward the end of *The Chalice and the Blade*. I was going to do *Breaking Free* and *Emergence*. I started to write *Breaking Free* and it came out rather academic, so I decided for the time being to put it aside. The academic has its place, but that's not what I wanted to do. There was, however, one chapter in *Breaking Free* that kept getting bigger and bigger, so I finally realized that this was the book I needed to write and it is the one I am now completing. It deals with intimate relations, sexuality, spirituality. It's an exciting book that has taken me into almost a complete history of intimate relations — not by themselves, but how they relate to what we have conventionally considered politics and economics.

Kind of like Foucault's *The History of Sexuality* or something like that?

Riane Eisler: Yes, in the sense that, like Foucault, I consider sexuality to be a social construct. No, in the sense that Foucault saw everything through a dominator lens, and I apply the templates of the partnership and dominator models to sexuality and spirituality. I deal with the human yearning for connection, and how the dominator model blocks it.

I didn't necessarily mean to bring up Foucault to debate his ideas, but in reference to the breadth of what he was attempting with that book. Is that the sort of framework?

Riane Eisler: It's broader in scope. It goes all the way back into protohistory. I do deal with the history of sexuality, and draw on some Foucault, but I am also interested in something he doesn't go into except in passing — the link between spirituality and sexuality, which is not a Foucault thing.

I understand. Again, I didn't mean to sidetrack us, but there have been surprisingly few books on your subject.

Riane Eisler: No, it's not at all surprising.

We talk about it all the time and there are thousands of books about sexuality. But in fact there have been very few that try to deal with it historically, so it sounds like yours will be apropos.
The other book?

Riane Eisler: The other book is on economics. Again, I'm applying the partnership and dominator models to economics. I am including things that most economists don't include: intrahousehold economics, for example. In other words, it's not just about that little narrow band that we consider economics, which is relations between men and men in commercial transactions, or between governments and governments. Or governments and corporations. That's just the middle band. I'm interested in taking it all the way from what happens in the household to what happens on the planet. Of course, that stuff in the middle is there, too. But there's a much broader scope, and again, partnership and dominator gender issues in economics, which have been ignored. It's incredible, really, when you consider that gender deals with the relations between the two halves of humanity.

Are there any other points that you think are important? I know it's hard to talk about yourself because it sounds like you're patting yourself on the back. But if someone picks up this book and starts to read it and says, "Who is this person? I've heard of the book but . . . ."

Riane Eisler: I should probably tell you one more thing that is important. It's my interest in evolution. I belong to a group called the General Evolution Research Group (known as GERG). David and I were among the founders of that group, and I was the only woman among them. My interest, as you saw in *The Chalice and the Blade*, was to explore whether there are isomorphisms — whether there are crossovers to cultural evolution from the very exciting systems- and chaos-theory approaches to biological evolution. This is an approach that does not just focus on how systems are, which is the Aristotelian approach. We study what is, but we also have a dynamic view, which is my approach: a nonlinear dynamic approach making it possible to see how systems change. And as you know from having read about my cultural transformation theory in *The Chalice and the Blade*, I found some extraordinary parallels in cultural evolution by applying that approach.

I'm glad you mentioned that because I was interested in your involvement with systems theory. It was spotting a reference in *The Chalice and the Blade* to Prigogine's and Stenger's *Order Out of Chaos*, which I had just read, that made me decide to read your book.

Riane Eisler: That connection is central to my work. I consider myself an evolutionary scholar or systems scholar. And, as I write in the introduction to *The Chalice and the Blade*, the problem with most of what is today called systems work, when you get into the social sciences part of it, is that it generally leaves out half of humanity. So if it's the study of chemistry by Prigogine, we're doing okay. But once you start going into the human arena, you have to ask yourself whether an approach that leaves out the female half of humanity is really a systems approach. Which is one reason I am trying to develop partnership studies.

I see partnership studies as a new integration. There has been a lot of complaining about the fragmentation of inquiry. But the way I look at it is from a systems standpoint. We had to have that fragmentation in order to break up a monolithic dominator view.

In order to present a really integrated view of knowledge in any field, particularly in a field dealing with human beings, you need a multidisciplinary approach. It's nonsensical to have politics and economics over here and then family relations over there (that is, if scholars even bother with family relations, except as a minor sidebar) then literature here and religion there, when they're all related. But to relate them again into different patterns, that's the challenge. Now this is where partnership studies, which are related in their approach to systems and chaos theory, come in. Theirs is a dynamic and inclusive approach. So I am a generalist. And I think we have to stress that this is a new type of scholarship that is still very suspect in academia.

Which is based on specialization.

Riane Eisler: Which is based on specialization, precisely. It's rough to be a generalist. For every chapter that I ever write—for example for this book that I'm now writing — I have to read something like twenty to fifty books. Obviously, I'm not an expert in any one of these fields. But my interest is in connections, relationships. And I mean that in two ways. In the first place, I'm very interested in the human yearning for connection. That's what I'm writing this one book about: the yearning for oneness through spirituality, the yearning for oneness through sexuality. I don't see them as all that different. In the second place, I'm also very interested in the connections between the various disciplines, and I see that as the future of scholarship. The big question is, will it again be only through the dominator prism? Or will what we teach as knowledge and truth now show that there is this other alternative?

DAVID LOYE

David, let's turn to you and what you're doing.

David Loye: In essence what I'm currently doing is applying the partnership and dominator models to the subject of moral sensitivity. We're at a juncture in evolution where we are caught up in a vast tangled ball of moral senselessness. Things just don't add up. We're lost, confused. It's very complex. But in the course of this exploration I've thought back on my own life, and maybe it's best to put my present work in this context. Contrasting my life with Riane's, our backgrounds couldn't be more radically different. Hers was this dramatic European background. Mine was, on the surface, a humdrum, Midwestern, good-old-boy, corn-fed American upbringing. But the image I think of was provided by Woody Allen in his movie *Annie Hall*: it's the WASP family from a Jewish viewpoint.

In the movie, Woody has a WASP girlfriend and he visits her WASP family back in the Midwest for Thanksgiving. It's a devastating portrait of the uptightness, the inhibition, the lack of emotionality, the inability to touch in such a family. It portrays the coolness of the WASP family in contrast to the Jewish family, the Italian family, or any of the more demonstrative backgrounds. Well, I grew up in that type of WASP family. I did not grow up as the angry young man. I grew up as the bewildered young man. I was bewildered by my family and when I went out the front door I was bewildered by the basic cruelty, immorality, and senselessness that hit me from the outside world. Looking back now, I see I was born a highly intelligent and sensitive organism, and over the first ten to twelve years of my life, before I learned the tricks of armoring, I was beaten down by the simple fact of living to a point where I thought I was actually subnormal in intelligence.

What did your parents do for a living?

David Loye: My father was an oil-company executive and my mother was a homemaker with myself and my two sisters to raise. But what I find so interesting in retrospect is that I see my early life was no different, essentially, from the lives of all the rest of us in the dominator system. We are all alike — even the toughest of us. We are at first little sea creatures without shells and the whole secret of our survival is to build those shells. I could not build my shell until I was about thirteen years old. I had a teacher then, Lucy Erickson in Bartlesville, Oklahoma. She spotted me as promising and encouraged me and that saved me. I think this is a familiar experience for both bewildered young men and angry young men — as well as bewildered young women and angry young women.

I see my life in retrospect as a series of roles that served as both armoring against the onslaught of the dominator world and as my modus operandi for dealing with that world. I also see the intellectual systems that we develop to account for how this is all put together — all the bad and all the good. We need some intelligible account to make sense of it.

Tell me about the roles.

David Loye: I shifted through an amazing number of them in my life and it was all part of providing a moving target: Don't let them get you. If they're beginning to move in on you, shift jobs, shift careers. Starting out in my teens, I was a factory worker, farmhand, bellhop, room-service waiter, oil-field worker. I was a shooter's helper on a seismograph crew, helping cram dynamite into shot holes in the oilfields in western Kansas. I went into the navy: World War II was there and so I served my country. After I came out of the navy and finished Dartmouth my first job was with the Mental Health Association during the infamous "snake pit" days. I then went into radio, where I was everything from janitor to writer, announcer, and newsman, to program director for a network radio station. Then I went into television when it first began.

You were in the Midwest . . .

David Loye: Still in Oklahoma. The most exciting thing in my early life was becoming a television writer and newsman in the early days. I was an aspiring television playwright and almost made it in those years with Kraft Theater and Studio One. Later I was one of the early *TV Guide* editors. All the time the role that held this all together, my super-armor, was that I thought I was going to be the writer of the "Great American Novel"and that all this shifting of occupations was just grist for my mill. I ground out Great American Novels on the side — none ever published, unfortunately — while doing all this other stuff. I started a tourist novelty business. I worked for government. I edited a number of magazines. Eventually I had a family with a wife and four kids and I was forced to move to New York City to make more money to put the kids through school. There I went to work for the largest, most evil public-relations agency in the world and from there became an account executive with an advertising agency on Madison Avenue. By now I was thirty-eight years old, with no connection to academia other than having long ago gone to Dartmouth and majored in psychology.

Why did you major in psychology? That's such a contrast to all your other occupations.

David Loye: I majored in psychology by accident. I went to Dartmouth because they offered a course in movie scriptwriting and I understood they also had what was known as the Irving Thalberg Memorial Library. I thought I could spend the college years just watching great movies and then go to Hollywood and make money to support my novel-writing. It turned out that the "library" consisted of nothing but some old moth-eaten scripts that Walter Wanger had donated and the "movie-writing" course was just a year of a handful of us gathering to tell dirty jokes and wait for an instructor who never showed up! The whole thing was a farce and I was forced to sign up to study something, so I picked psychology as a major.

But this, in turn, led me to my first great intellectual attachment, to Freud. My other early attachments were to Marx and the great activist theologian Reinhold Niebuhr. These attachments, over time, proved to be pivotal, but meanwhile there I was all these years later, a captive in the business world. I found myself in early middle-age, thirty-eight years old, and going down the drain. I had become a ghostwriter and editor. I wrote a lot of speeches, articles, and other copy, and edited books for people, and everything I wrote or edited bore the signature of somebody else. I was depersonalized. I was beaten down by the dominator system, so I decided to fight back and get out of it.

I went back to graduate school at nights after a full workday. I had been a social activist and also, to the extent possible, a reformer in the government and business worlds. I had the vision of developing an action theory — that is, theory as a guide for action — that might do some good in this messed-up world by updating Marx and Freud in modern humanistic terms. It took me ten years at the New School for Social Research, but I got my doctorate and right off the bat taught at Princeton and moved to the faculty of the U.C.L.A. School of Medicine.

So this was a rather dramatic change from everything I'd ever done before. For a while I regretted all those years of academic learning I had lost out on during my wayward youth. I felt so ignorant at first, and isolated. No one in all the generations of my family before me had been an academic or gained a doctorate. But, as it turned out, everything in the series of armoring roles that led up to this point provided me with a much greater understanding of how the world is really put together at all levels — government, business, crime. As a journalist, for example, I had worked closely with the police in trying to keep the Mafia out of Oklahoma and was the first television newsman to film a murder trial from within the courtroom. Having a family was even more important. Had I originally gone on to graduate school and not had my daughters Jenella and Kate and sons Chris and Jonathan, both my life and my experience would have been greatly impoverished, for through them and my first wife I learned love.

So when I finally became a social scientist I had a much greater understanding of how the world was put together than I would have had I just followed the normal academic track. For that I'm everlastingly grateful. My work background was valuable, for example, when I became a research professor at the U.C.L.A. School of Medicine and had my earlier television experience to draw on in carrying out the biggest study that had yet been done of the effects of television on adults.

When was this study done?

David Loye: It was done from 1972 through 1978. I wrote an article about it for *Psychology Today* and other articles for professional journals. But let me shift to my next role.

Before I joined the Princeton faculty I wrote my first book. This was *The Healing of a Nation*, a study of 350 years of American black and white history using history as the casebook for what I called the "black and white sickness." I applied psychology and sociology to identifying the symptoms, causes, and workings of racism, as well as cures for it. Fired up by the Rodney King verdict and the Los Angeles uprising, I'm working on a new version of this book now. It was a national award winner on racism when it came out. Somehow I managed to write it at the same time I was working full time, going to school at night, and dealing with all the complexity of life with a large family. I don't know how I did it, in retrospect.

I always thought of my second book as being an attempt to supply the missing psychology for the better part of Marx and Engels, by which I do *not* mean that dumb dominator idea of the "dictatorship of the proletariat." This book was called *The Leadership Passion: A Psychology of Ideology.* It was an empirical study of left, right, and middle—of liberal-conservative dynamics and how this left/right interaction actually was a major driving force accounting for the twists and turns of history.

Then I became a futurist and wrote a book called *The Knowable Future: A Psychology of Forecasting and Prophecy,* on how we use the brain and the mind to predict the future. That was followed by my most popular book, *The Sphinx and the Rainbow: Brain, Mind, and Future Vision,* which went into a number of foreign editions.

Along in there I met Riane. I want to come back to that, but first let me briefly sketch the shifting not of roles but of mindsets I was involved in over this time. I think this is important because the readers of this book, almost to the last man and woman, will all be caught up in this business of shifting their own intellectual systems, looking for the framework that at last puts it all in place. This we *must* do if we are to survive in the dominator system. And we *must* break out of it!

What was your first framework of this sort?

David Loye: Well, I'm not sure it was first, but it is still vivid. Bartlesville, Oklahoma, where I grew up, was a company town for Cities Service and Phillips Petroleum oil companies. It was the most socially and racially stratified town imaginable. I grew up the child of members of the Republican country-club set, my dad being an oil executive. The whole town had a primarily protofascist orientation — this was one of the rare towns actually to experience rightist book burnings around the time of World War II. People stormed the library and took out whatever they didn't like. Yet for some reason I grew up turned wholly against the classism and racism and the country-club set of my upbringing. At the age of fifteen or so I began to fight automatically for Roosevelt and the New Deal against my father and any other grown-up I felt up to confronting in those days. In retrospect, I have never really understood why.

Because I grew up in a Christian setting, it was Christianity that first gave me a worldview for explaining what it was all about. I ran into the inevitable problems with that view and was tremendously relieved to find Freud. I dropped Christianity, translated all my Christian concepts into Freudian concepts, and thought, "This is it, the final place." But once again, as time went on, I found all the problems with Freud. As an undergraduate at Dartmouth, but much more so later at the New School, when sociology was my minor, I came to know the work of Marx and Engels. This was a gripping framework, but once again there were all the problems.

So then my mind became the kind of eclectic mush that is the mind-set for social scientists and the rest of us, where you've got Marx, Max Weber, Émile Durkheim, and Vilfredo Pareto on the sociology side, and you've got Freud, Jung, Abraham Maslow, and many others on the psychological side, and you have this glorious free-floating thing in your head that protects you. It's all armoring against the onslaught of this dominator system that is continually trying to beat you under and keep you enslaved.

The most dramatic change in my life, intellectually as well as emotionally, came after I met Riane. I began to absorb her cultural transformation theory, this framework for twenty-five thousand years of our cultural evolution, and the dominator model versus the partnership model, and to see what a magnificent job she had done of tying it all together for the first time. This was really the most powerful intellectual experience for me, because through working with her, I began to see, with increasing excitement, what was emerging from this manuscript she was writing. Hey, I thought, this is really greater in its own way than Marx, greater than Freud, and part of the reason is that for the first time thinking at this level is including the experience and perspective of *women* as well as men. And for the first time this is a truly scientific systems view, embracing prehistory as well as history. She had a much greater data base to draw on than Freud, Marx, or even Darwin, to whom her work has been compared. But only a woman could have written this book, and I think it's a historical contribution of a major order.

How did you meet Riane?

David Loye: I was at U.C.L.A. and she lived nearby. At first we were in love and extremely taken with each other and each other's work. We discovered that we were talking on increasingly higher intellectual, emotional, and aesthetic levels when she got involved in writing this unknown book. It was this great galloping manuscript that she was despairing over every so often. Would she ever get it published? Could she even *finish* it? After I began to read it I was in there saying this is tremendous and you *will* finish it and you *will* publish it, even when I wasn't sure myself.

When was that actually?

David Loye: It was roughly from 1977 to 1987, when the book was finally published. When I first met Riane I gave up a lot of the things I was doing at U.C.L.A. because she was seriously ill and I felt that I had to intervene to help her with her health. Later, we became involved in the General Evolution Research Group. This had an important effect on us as we were both moving rapidly into systems science, the logical discipline for us because of the breadth of our experiences and our intellectual interests. It was, however, another inadequate framework because, as with much of social science, it was not a true systems science at all; it was male-centered and mechanistic. Yet it was the only discipline then that really offered us a home. With systems philosopher Ervin Laszlo and others we co-founded this international group of scholars from Italy, France, Great Britain, Russia, Austria, and Hungary and began to meet in places all around Europe.

You started to tell me something about your work in moral sensitivity.

David Loye: That, other than my feeling for Riane, is now the all-consuming passion of my life. We're going to waste this planet and wipe ourselves out if we go on letting the rightist fundamentalists co-opt the idea of morals and morality for their own. Based on systems science, brain research, chaos theory, archaeology, and a host of other fields, my work shows that we're approaching a bifurcation point not only for scientific, psychological, social, political, and economic systems, but also for the kind of activist spirituality that is rooted in moral sensitivity.

Bifurcation point?

David Loye: I call it an evolutionary door in time, for this is really what it is. To simplify radically, on one side of this door that after millions of years of evolution is looming before us is the old dominator consciousness of the rightists, sexists, racists, and mechanistic science. On the other side of this evolutionary door in time lies a future of partnership moral sensitivity. Caught up in this project to the extent that I can hardly sleep or eat at times, I have over the past several years written the bulk of at least five books. Now I have to polish them and find a publisher — which is not easy these days, when so many people shy away from "morality" because of the rightist pollution and the impression that morality is something old-fashioned and uptight. In fact, within the evolutionary perspective, given our capability of smothering ourselves in overpopulation, destroying the environment and the ozone layer, or blowing ourselves up, what's involved here at the core — moral sensitivity — is literally a matter of life or death.

What about your involvement in the partnership movement?

David Loye: That has been quite a roller-coaster ride. There was a tremendous readership response to *The Chalice and the Blade*. We co-founded a Center for Partnership Studies. This helped spawn Centers for Partnership Education in thirty-two states throughout the U.S., as well as in the Seychelles Islands, Greece, and Argentina as of the last count. Most recently — as you know so well from having been there — activity for this movement-in-the-making led to people from forty countries, the majority of them *The Chalice and the Blade* readers, pouring into Crete for the First International Minoan Celebration of Partnership. It's an amazing and heartening development that gives us — as well as thousands of other people — hope for the future.

Any final thoughts?

David Loye: I guess the only other thing I would add is that this all seems to follow the old dialectical Hegelian and synergistic pattern of an interaction that produces something greater than what either interactor could have produced alone. It's the dynamics of partnership really — the essence of what Riane and I are both trying to share with others. Through living together, through our separate and joint work, through experiencing the growth of this partnership movement that is very slowly spreading, we are gradually being lifted to levels that are light years beyond our original capacities. When we were younger neither of us could have visualized or begun to handle what we can now. I think also that had we never met, neither one of us would have come this far. This tremendous interaction between the two of us has been the greatest experience of our lives.

One result of re-examining human society from a gender-holistic perspective has been a new theory of cultural evolution. This theory, which I have called Cultural Transformation theory, proposes that underlying the great surface diversity of human culture are two basic models of society. ... [T]he *dominator* model is what is popularly termed either patriarchy or matriarchy — the *ranking* of one half of humanity over the other. The second, in which social relations are primarily based on the principle of *linking* rather than ranking, may best be described as the *partnership* model. In this model — beginning with the most fundamental difference in our species, between male and female — diversity is not equated with either inferiority or superiority.

Resources

Bifurcation point: The point in a process or system where deterministic laws are no longer operant and where certain predictability of outcome is impossible. Instability, chance, the breakdown of order are all characteristic of this nonetheless inevitable component of all systems and processes.

Chaos theory: An attempt to organize inquiry into natural phenomena that defy explanation by Newtonian, Einsteinian, or even quantum physics. It deals with complex systems (such as weather or population), and within them focuses on the breakdown of order, the influence of chance, and the perpetual self-organization of systems independent of the mechanistic laws of dynamics and thermodynamics. It embodies a critique of Cartesian and Newtonian rationalism and physics. It stresses the interrelatedness and interdependence of all motion in the universe and, furthermore, the potentially enormous effects that relatively small events can have on relatively large systems over great spans of time and space.

Cultural transformation theory: The central thesis of this theory is that the direction of the cultural evolution for dominator and partnership societies is very different. It views the process of evolution as not simply linear or technologic but instead involving great shifts that have actually happened quite rapidly and comprehensively, literally transforming whole cultures and societies. It shares many aspects of the chaos theory applied to human evolution (bifurcation points, self-organization, etc.) but specifically includes the interaction between male and female halves of humanity and examines social processes inclusive of — in fact, focusing on — the most basic components of our social relations: men and women, parents and children, family structures, socialization processes, etc.

Deconstructionism: Impossible to define "objectively" since it is neither a scientific term nor is there one definition shared by the very groups (academics, literary critics, artists, and intellectuals, among others) that use it with the frequency of common parlance. It refers to a method of taking apart existing paradigms or systems of thought (including itself!) and demonstrating the socially constructed basis of them. It is concerned with revealing the interests of the parties (such as priests and doctors) to the creation and perpetuation of myths and social norms. It focuses on the manipulation of sign and symbol in the manufacture of power, particularly the use of language and the hierarchization of discourse (e.g., "science is the master discourse").

Makhno: Nestor I. Makhno was a revolutionary anarchist. He led guerrilla forces in the Ukraine during the period of the Russian Revolution, combating both the Red and White armies. Eventually defeated, he went into exile.

Mondragon: Begun forty years ago in the Basque town of the same name, Mondragon is a network of more than 170 worker cooperatives serving over one hundred thousand people. Its many productive activities include banking, technical assistance, research and design organizations, stores, and appliance-manufacturing. Mondragon survived Franco's repression, and continues to thrive today.

Nucleations: The mechanisms by which fluctuations are diffused throughout an entire region or space. This is a term commonly used in chemistry to describe a key part of the process of, for example, the movement from a liquid to a vaporous state. How it applies to complex systems such as social organization may be essential to understanding how stability arises out of the breakdown of structure.

Strange attractors: Physicists have used the term *attractor* to mean either a fixed point or limit cycle representing behavior that has reached a steady state or repeated itself continuously. This implies predictability, perpetual self-replication, order. But in deep turbulence (chaotic, "noisy" systems), a phenomenon appears both theoretically and in the real world that suggests a different kind of pattern. This pattern allows for the possibility of an infinite line in a finite space, a loop that never repeats exactly but that loops nonetheless. Since there is no fixed point or repeating cycle to this process, the attractor involved is called *strange*. The term's extrapolation from physics to social phenomena identifies a subtle force that defines parameters in time and space within or around which complex systems align themselves. The term has come under fire and become more widely used precisely because of its "mystical" properties. After all, *strange*, by definition, means unexpected, unpredictable, different from a norm.

— MATHEW CALLAHAN

Suggested Readings

Luis Buñuel. *My Last Sigh*. New York: Vintage, 1984.

Judy Chicago. *The Dinner Party*. Garden City, NY: Doubleday, 1979.

James DeMeo. "The Origins and Diffusion of Patrism in Saharasia, c. 4000 BCE: Evidence for a Worldwide Climate-Linked Geographical Pattern in Human Behavior." *World Futures: The Journal of General Evolution*, 1991, vol. 30, pp. 247-271.

Umberto Eco. *The Name of the Rose*. New York: Warner, 1988.

Riane Eisler. *The Chalice and the Blade*. HarperSanFrancisco, 1987.

Riane Eisler and David Loye. *The Partnership Way*. HarperSanFrancisco, 1990.

Friedrich Engels. *The Origins of the Family, Private Property, and the State*. New York: International Publishers, 1972.

Karen Finley. *Shock Treatment*. San Francisco: City Lights, 1990.

Michel Foucault. *The History of Sexuality*. New York: Random House, 1980.

Emma Goldman. *Living My Life*. New York: Dover, 1930.

_____. *The Traffic in Women*. Ojai, CA: Times Change Press, 1970.

Alexandra Kollontai. *Workers Opposition*. Seattle, WA: Left Bank (n.d.).

Peter Kropotkin. *Anarchism* and *Anarchist Communism* (two essays). London: Freedom Press, 1987.

Ervin Laszlo. *Evolution: The Grand Synthesis*. Boston: Shambhala, 1987.

Richard Leakey. *Origins Reconsidered: In Search of What Makes Us Human*. New York: Doubleday, 1992.

Richard Leakey and Roger Lewin. *Origins*. New York: Viking Penguin, 1991.

Kurt Lewin. *A Dynamic Theory of Personality: Selected Papers*. Tr. by D.K. Adams and K.E. Zener. London: McGraw-Hill, 1935.

_____. *Field Theory in Social Science*. Westport, CT: Greenwood, 1975.

Filippo T. Marinetti. *The Futurist Manifesto* (in *Selected Writings*. New York: Farrar, Straus & Giroux, 1972.)

Paul MacLean. *The Triune Brain in Evolution: Role in Paleocerebral Functions*. New York: Plenum Press, 1990.

David F. Noble. *A World Without Women*. New York: Knopf, 1992.

Ilya Prigogine and Isabelle Stengers. *Order Out of Chaos*. New York: Bantam, 1984.

Pierre J. Proudhon. *General Idea of the Revolution in the Nineteenth Century*. UK: Pluto Press, 1989.

Mary Shelley. *Frankenstein, Or the Modern Prometheus*. Chicago: University of Chicago Press, 1982.

CONNECTIONS

If you want to know more about the Center for Partnership Studies co-founded by Riane Eisler and David Loye, the Centers for Partnership Education throughout the U.S., the international partnership movement, or about membership in the artists' collective Komotion International and the magazine *Komotion International Live & Kicking*, here's how to get in touch:

For information about CPEs in the United States, the Seychelles Islands, Argentina, and Crete, and how to become involved in the partnership movement globally, write to The Center for Partnership Studies, Dept. A, P.O. Box 51936, Pacific Grove CA 93923.

For membership and subscription information about Komotion International, write to Komotion International, P.O. Box 410502, San Francisco CA 94141-0502, or call (415) 861-6423.

Selections from the catalog of

Times Change Press

The Traffic in Women and other essays on feminism by Emma Goldman; with a biography by Alix Kates Shulman
Emma Goldman was a dynamic anarchist whose feminism differed markedly from that of her suffrage-oriented contempo-raries. Because divisions between liberal and radical approaches to women's liberation are still not resolved, her essays have an uncanny relevancy to problems now being dealt with. 8th print-ing 1990. ISBN 0-87810-001-6 *Illustrated; 63 pp; $4.25*

How Deep Is Deep Ecology? with an essay-review on **Woman's Freedom** by George Bradford
A veteran social/environmental activist critiques some deep-ecology writings and posits a close relationship between freedom for women and the salvation of the earth. 1st printing 1989. ISBN 0-87810-035-0 *Illustrated; 94 pp; $5.50*

Free Space: A Perspective on the Small Group in Women's Liberation by Pamela Allen
This is an excellent handbook for people wondering how to begin or restructure the small group, used by many people as a way of relating to different needs. 3d printing. ISBN 0-87810-006-7 *Illustrated; 64 pp; $4.25*

Living with Purpose When the Gods Are Gone by Robert P. Crosby
Five lucid essays show readers the way to creating their own set of ethical values, or "core moralities," based on clearer knowledge of self and the world. Includes a brief study guide. 1st printing 1991. ISBN 0-87810-038-5 *Illustrated; 64 pp; $5.95*

Some Pictures from My Life: A Diary by Marcia Salo Rizzi
This diary/dream journal reflects the author's own particular struggles and at the same time says much about the lives of all women. (The author is the creator of our "Womanbirth" poster.) ISBN 0-87810-022-9 *Illustrated; 64 pp; $3.25*

UNBECOMING MEN: A Men's Consciousness-Raising Group Writes on Oppression and Themselves
This book reflects the struggles of a group of men who came together because of their increasingly unavoidable awareness of sexism. 9th printing. ISBN 0-87810-015-6 *Illustrated; 64 pp; $4.25*

POSTERS (17 x 22 inches)

Womanbirth: "I am Woman Giving Birth to Myself"; $2.95
Che Guevara: "Let me say, at the risk of seeming ridiculous, that the true revolutionary is guided by great feelings of love"; $2.95

* * *

TIMES CHANGE PRESS is a noncommercial, nondoctrinaire press dedicated to radical change in opposition to the greediness of political and economic power, of environmental and human exploitation, and to the domination of one gender, ethnic, or sexual orientation over another.

Times change and with them their possibilities; times change and with them their demands — I CHING

To order direct, send payment (including $1.50 postage and handling for the first item, 75¢ for each additional item: minimum total $5) to Times Change Press, Publishers Services, P. O. Box 2510, Novato CA 94948. Orders for California delivery add 7.25% sales tax. **Toll-free number for VISA/MasterCard orders only: 800-488-8595.**

Outside U.S.A.: Add 30% and round to the nearest dollar. Payment in U.S. dollars payable at U.S. bank. Surface postage is included.

Quality bookstores stock our titles. Prices are subject to change.